I0752515

FINISHING LINE PRESS
www.finishinglinepress.com

Night Breaks in the Garret

Poems and Peregrinations

עלות-הלילה אויפֿן בוידעם

לידער און רײַזעס

by

Yermiyahu Ahron Taub

Finishing Line Press
Georgetown, Kentucky

Night Breaks in the Garret

עלות-הלילה אויפֿן בוידעם

ISBN 979-8-89990-417-2 First Edition

Publisher: Leah Huete de Maines
Editor: Christen Kincaid
Cover Art: Joshua Meyer, *Edge of the Evening*, Oil on canvas, 2024, 40 x 36 inches
© Joshua Meyer
Interior Art: Page 45: *Diner Counter Jukebox*, credit: nano; Page 67: *Rachel's Tomb, Near Bethlehem*, credit: clu
Author Photo: Paul Schaper
Cover Design: Elizabeth Maines McCleavy

Order online: www.finishinglinepress.com
also available on amazon.com

Author inquiries and mail orders:
Finishing Line Press
PO Box 1626
Georgetown, Kentucky 40324
USA

Contents

I. Dusk's Dawn: Droplets Dotting Damask

Entreaty (English and Yiddish) 2
What the Muzak Presaged ... and Provided 6
The Light at the Beginning of the Tunnel (English and Yiddish) 8
Shadow Box, Rustle Thunder 12
Stasis at the Interstices 14
Portamento, Prayer 16
The Babe's Legacy 19
Crash Course in the Classics 21
Ardor in and out of the Catacombs 23
City of Sweets 25
Village Tableau, Far From the Parade 27
Polemic on Pallor and Parchment 29
Activist's Retreat 31
Mirage No. 2 33
Permanent Resident, Without Green Card 35
Glass Dreams 37
Night of Seroconversion and Aftermath/Dialogue, in Eternal Embryo ... 39
Rendezvous Fantasia (English and Yiddish) 43
Throne, with Cat (English and Yiddish) 48
Fellow Travelers (English and Yiddish) 52

II. Black Blots Blast into Blue Baklava

Litany/ies: October, Long Past Millennium's Turn 56
(Fraternal) Twin Meditations on the Theme of Tenacity 59
Bebop Blues/Lullaby Ghost 61
Milk and Honey Moon Harvest (English and Yiddish) 65

Midrash on a Gravestone Acrostic Inscription (English and Yiddish) 70
Peace/Pieces of Mind 76
Water, Rising 78
Three's a Minyan 80
Siesta's Sustenance 83
M and M and the Queen Greet the S Queen 85
(Not Entirely) New World Rituals 87
Unanswered Questions Around the Endemic Bend 89
Object Lessons/Treasure, Retained 91
What the Babushkas Saw 94
A Summons in Spring 97
Plain Plenty: Blossom, Bounty, Betty 100
Ignorance, Bliss 103
Flaneur of the Fields 105
Hole(s) in the Wall/Shelter Island 108
At Last, a Celebration, Or, Improvisations on the Question of Inspiration (English and Yiddish) 110
Along the Path of Peppermint Pillows: Notes to My Readers 116

Acknowledgments 119
About the Author 122

For Paul Schaper
loving friendship
lo all these years

I. Dusk's Dawn:
Droplets Dotting Damask

Entreaty

Father calls me every week,
driven by a force beyond himself.
He implores me to prayer,
to study—with him, with anyone—
to a lecture, to hear tell of ethics and Torah.
My silence is no deterrent.
It's for your own good, he insists,
for the good of the people of Israel.

Father calls me to keep *Shabes*,
to put aside the texts in their thorniness,
all the prohibitions in their variety.
Those can come later.
Light the candles,
recite the *Kiddush*, relish *tsholnt*.
Rejoice in the rest of our Holy Day.
Even just that.

Father calls me to marriage,
suggests the granddaughter of his second wife,
laments my wifelessness and childlessness,
remains indifferent to my passion, my self,
despite having known for more than twenty years:
no matter those.
No man shall be without a woman.
No man shall abandon the imperative to be fruitful and multiply.

Mother passed over when I was young.
Her body was plucked, riven, her essence crushed by
the impasse in communication, the inadequacy of words,
the clash between piety and romance,
asceticism and beauty. Bereft of shelter from the enormity of his
disappointment in me, I reach for the skirts of her ghostly gown.
With all of these white hairs,
I ought to know better.

Only these words can save me.
Only your attention, however fleeting, can halt this spiral.
Is that you I see between the pines?
Only the melody of the nightingale, the grace of deer in the clearing,
only my step, however tentative on the leaves of this forest path,
can stem the grief, hovering, patient, that threatens to engulf me.
Please: stay not away.
Walk with me

and with our doe alongside.

נאָר די ווערטער קענען מיך ראַטעווען.
נאָר דײַן אויפֿמערק, כאָטש פֿאַרבײַגעיינדיק, קען אויפֿהערן דעם ספּיראַל.
צי זע איך טאַקע דיך צווישן די סאָסנעס?
נאָר דער ניגון פֿונעם סאָלאָוויי, די גראַציעזקייט פֿון הירשן אין דער פּאָליאַנע,
נאָר מײַן טראָט, כאָטש טענטאַטיוו, אויף די בלעטער פֿון דער וואַלד-סטעזשקע,
קען פֿאַרהאַלטן דעם טרויער, וואַרטנדיק, געדולדיק, וואָס סטראַשעט מיך פֿאַרשלינגען.
זײַ אַזוי גוט: בלײַב ניט אַוועק.
קום מיט מיר צו גיין

און מיט אונדזער סאַרנע דערבײַ.

געבעט

דער טאַטע קלינגט מיך אָן יעדן וואָך,
גערודפֿט פֿון אַ כּוח שטאַרקער ווי ער אַליין.
ער בעט מיך דאַווענען,
לערנען זיך—מיט אים, מיט ווער עס זאָל ניט זיין—
צו אַ שיעור, צו הערן אַ דבֿר-תּורה, אַ וואָרט מוסר.
מײַן שווײַגעניש איז ניט קיין אָפּהאַלט.
ס'איז פֿאַר דײַן טובֿה, שפּאַרט ער זיך אײַן,
לטובֿת כּלל-ישׂראל.

דער טאַטע רופֿט מיך צו היטן שבת,
אָוועקצולייגן די ספֿרים מיט זייערע שוועריקייטן,
די כּלרליי מיני מצוות לא-תעשׂה.
זיי קענען שפּעטער קומען.
צינד אָן די ליכט,
מאַך קידוש, האָט הנאה פֿון טשאָלנט.
פֿריי זיך אין דער מנוחה פֿונעם יום-הקודש.
כאָטש נאָר דאָס.

דער טאַטע רופֿט מיך צו חתונה,
לייגט ער פֿאָר דעם אייניקל פֿון זײַן צווייטער פֿרוי,
באַווייַנט מײַן פֿרוילאָזיקייט און קינדלאָזיקייט,
בלײַבט גלײַכגילטיק צו מײַן פּאַסיע, דעם איך-גופֿא,
כאָטש ער ווייסט וועגן זיי שוין מער ווי צוואַנציק יאָר:
מאַכט ניט אויס.
אַ מאַן טאָר ניט זײַן אָן אַ פֿרוי.
אַ מאַן טאָר ניט פֿאַרלאָזן דעם חיובֿ פֿון פּרו ורבֿו.

די מאַמע איז אַוועק ווען איך בין יונג געווען.
איר גוף איז געווען געפּליקט, צעריסן, איר גײַסט צעשטעטערט פֿונעם
אימפּאַס אין קאָמוניקאַציע, דוחק פֿון ווערטער,
צונויפשטויס צווישן פֿרומקייט און ראָמאַנס,
אַסקעטיקייט און שיינקייט. אָן אַן אָפּדאַך פֿונעם אומגעהײַערקייט פֿון זײַן
אַנטוישונג אין מיר דערלאַנג איך צו די קליידלעך
פֿון איר שדישן באַלקלייד.
מיט אַזויפיל ווײַסע האָר
זאָל איך בעסער וויסן.

What the Muzak Presaged ... and Provided

The soundscape was running its seemingly endless course, having blanched its source material of locomotive and saffron, well, of everything, really, leaving the composition a husk, a skeleton in flight from its medical alcove, somehow funneled to flow and grate into the ears and onto the nerves of the patients waiting to undergo examinations, then consultations they knew not would be hopeful, neutral, or dire. After all, why should the Muzak care? What cares of its own did the Muzak have, when all it had to do was follow the funnel and flow and gyrate and grate, finding its target in those who resisted soothing, whose nerves were now electric with exhaustion and edge, whose teeth were clenched, whose nails were bitten down to their moons, whose hairs on nape were standing at attention.

Only he was not one of those thus affected because he didn't know the original source material and so couldn't wince at its blanching, and because the doctor he was about to see was his yeshiva friend's father. And he had spent many a Sabbath afternoon in their home that was lined, indeed overflowing (from shelves but never onto floors), with holy books, and graced by a black cat, who, like all domestic animals, had to be fed before humans, as the sages required, as his friend told him. And on Sunday afternoons, too, with his friend's sisters as they all created sand art layers of aqua and yellow and green and fuchsia, the visual antithesis of Muzak, abstract and varied and luminous and fragile so don't shake them!

And so he was relaxed or at least trying to be watching the sun struggle past the clouds and the broad Venetian blinds with their burgundy connective strips. He had already had spectacles for a number of years, was not a stranger to the darkened room to come, with its black letters shining back at him from the illuminated panel. Until they shone no more having diminished to more-than-specks and then just to specks. Until his friend's father asked "This one or *this* one?" and sometimes he could barely tell, for the difference was so minute, itself microscopic.

When he heard a broadcaster of news interrupt stop altogether the muzak, speak of a mysterious disease spreading among his people, a morsel, a tidbit barely bigger than the specks on the wall on whose parameters he was about to be tested, for he knew even then that they were his people, had always known that ever since he had had to look away in the locker room so he wouldn't glimpse the athletic magnificence of some of his yeshiva mates given the visibility of their effect on him so they wouldn't see his eyes on them so they wouldn't see him trying not to look at them trying but failing so desperately to look away

and he wondered if this disease would find him seek him out hunt him down spotting him in the crowd not that he was hard to spot, in a crowd or outside of one, with his willowy form and lilac voice, he would not be a difficult target to locate and what could he possibly do to resist, to protect himself, other than make himself smaller than he already was which was already really quite small and hope and plead and pray and work to avoid this that sought to eradicate him when he was only just barely a man as defined by his people, his other original people. And all he could do was mumble his way through his examination, hoping the terror was not marked on him and when he finally did make it through with a new prescription and thanked the doctor and found his way shivering to the exit

he hoped it that is the plague with its lesions and fevers wasn't in pursuit with the figure in the hooded black cloak not far behind and that these shivers now weren't themselves markers that his foray into fever dream (for that was all it had ever been) was nearing its end and he feared that all of his sinful lusting after his athletic yeshiva mates had already wreaked this terrible havoc and that the plague with its finality and indifference and ravenousness would not be stopped would not spare him or others like him

and when he was finally home beneath the covers and the images of his classmates did not this once visit him (for he could not allow them) then the river currents of Muzak returned to him embraced enveloped and rescued him and he was so glad for them for the gift of their blank … and brief … respite

The Light at the Beginning of the Tunnel

I walk down the corridor past a closed door;
light leaks out from beneath.
I speculate about the activities of the person behind it.
Is he listening to music on headphones?
Perhaps Vivaldi. Perhaps heavy metal.
Is he watching television on mute,
the colors from the screen illuminating his night face,
the images dancing over his indifference to
or unawareness of my presence?
Perhaps he's reading *The New Yorker*
or an underground comic.

I follow footsteps with trepidation:
the movement of …
let's call him the man from the bar.
Why am I here? Why did I get into the car? Why tonight?
How did my inexperience become unbearable, repugnant even?
Why didn't I give him my number and meet him
for cappuccino and biscotti at another time, in another place?
Why did I follow him from that watering hole in the wall?
These questions swarm around me unanswered, unanswerable.
And still I move forward, following him,
to the threshold of the sham Eden at corridor's end.

The man from the bar is now above me.
How fine he is, refined even, chiseled in a glow so delicate
he insists it must not be obscured.
The invasion begins without an opening volley.
I beseech, my white flag frantically aflutter.
My cries ricochet off his resolve.
He tells me to shut up, stop struggling.
I obey, float above myself, in the nether region
between witness and onlooker. If I don't …
He proceeds methodically, relentlessly …
until suddenly, finally it's over. Or is it?

In the morning,
he returns me to my basement without banter,
deposits me on my doorstep.
Now he knows where I live.
I wonder again about his housemate.
Did he hear? Surely this was not the first time
pleading prospered in that room.
Perhaps I should be fortunate he didn't partake. At least that.
Below ground, I dab in vain at the blood—my virginal secretion—
and entomb myself under covers for days,
under shrouds for decades.

אין דער פֿרי
נעמט ער מיך אין מײַן קעלער צוריק אָן רעדערײַ,
שטעלט מיך אויפֿן שוועל.
איצט ווייסט ער ווו איך ווױן.
כוווּנדער זיך ווידער וועגן זײַן מיטוווינער.
האָט ער געהערט? זיכער איז דאָס ניט דאָס ערשטע מאָל
טענהות האָבן זיך צעבליט אין זײַן מיטווױנערס שטוב.
ס'איז מיר אפֿשר אַ מזל וואָס ער האָט זיך ניט באַטייליקט. לכל-הפּחות דאָס.
אונטער דער ערד טו איך דאָס בלוט אומזיסט אַ שמיר—דעם בתולישן אויסשייד—
און קבֿר זיך אײַן אונטער קאָלדערעס טעג לאַנג,
אונטער תּכריכים יאָרצענדליקער לאַנג.

די ליכט בײַם אָנהייב פֿונעם טונעל

כ'גיי דורך אַ קאָרידאָר פֿאַרבײַ אַ פֿאַרמאַכטער טיר;
פֿון אונטן רינט אַרויס ליכט.
כ'פֿרעג זיך וועגן די טוּונגען פֿונעם מענטשן הינטער איר.
צי הערט ער צו מיט הערערס צו מוזיק?
אפֿשר וויוואַלדי. קאָן זײַן מעטאַלראָק.
צי קוקט ער אויף אַ טעלעוויזיע וואָס איז פֿאַרשטילט,
אינעם עקראַנס קאָלירן זײַן נאַכט-פּנים באַלויכט,
די אימאַזשן צעטאַנצן זיך איבער זײַן גלײַכגילט
אָדער ניט-וויסן פֿון מײַן זײַן הי?
קאָן זײַן ער לייענט דער *ניו-יאָרקער*
אָדער אַן "אונטערערדישן" קאָמיק.

כ'גיי נאָך נאָך זײַנע טריט מיט ציטערניש:
דער באַוועג פֿון ...
לאָמיר אים אָנרופֿן דעם מאַן פֿונעם באַר.
צו וואָס בין איך אַהער? פֿאַר וואָס אינעם אויטאָ אַרײַן? וואָס עפּעס הײַנט אויף דער נאַכט?
ווי איז מײַן אומגעניטקייט געוואָרן ניט צו פֿאַרטראָגן, חלשות אפֿילו?
פֿאַר וואָס ניט געגעבן דעם טעלעפֿאָן-נומער און זיך געטראָפֿן
אויף קאַפּוטשינאָ און ביסקאָטי אַן אַנדערט מאָל, אין אַן אַנדער אָרט?
פֿאַר וואָס האָב איך אים נאָכגעגאַנגען פֿון אָט דער קנײַפּיע?
די קשוית קישען אַרום זיך, ניט געלייזט, אומגעלייזטע.
און דאָך גיי איך ווײַטער, גיי איך אים נאָך,
צום שוועל פֿונעם פֿאַלשן גן-עדן בײַם קאָרידאָרס סוף.

דער מאַן פֿונעם באַר איז איצט איבער מיר.
ווי פֿײַן איז ער, צו מאָל ראַפֿינירט, ציזעלירט אין אַ גלימער אַזש דעליקאַט
אויף וואָס ער באַשטייט זאָל ניט ווערן פֿאַרדעקט.
די אינוואַזיע פֿאַנגט זיך אָן אָן אַן ערשטן שאָס.
איך בעט זיך, די ווײַסע פֿאָן מײַנע פֿלאַטערט זיך ווילד.
די געשרייען ריקאָשעטירן אַראָפּ פֿון זײַן פֿעסטקייט.
ער הייסט מיך פֿאַרשווײַגן, אויפֿהערן זיך ראַנגלען.
איך פֿאָלג, שוועב איבער זיך, אינעם נידער-ראַיאָן
צווישן עדות און בײַשטייער. אויב ניט ...
ער איז ממשיך אויף אַ מעטאָדאָלאָגישן אופֿן, אומרחמנותדיק ...
ביז עס איז פּלוצעם, סוף־כּל־סוף, פֿאַרענדיקט. צי איז עס?

Shadow Box, Rustle Thunder

The satellite radio station or web broadcast or app or maybe a mix, he never was quite certain, blasted songs that gushed growl and cacophony and crash. The men—the gods in training—grunted and heaved and sweat. They leaned over one another as they exchanged "spotting" favors and words of encouragement, bulge above face, within reach of iron and finger. The plates clattered against each other when restacked, supplementing the din. Some wiped down the benches, but the smells of their collective efforts lingered in the air for decades, a potency impossible to eradicate. Their chests had no need to burst forth from impossible tank tops; they simply flowered beneath. Undaunted, the "skinny" calves would not be denied, insisting, too, upon admiration. Here was fruit to be measured, weighed, and appraised before the hard-to-please mirrors. Here, then, a cornucopia for all of the senses. Before the booths of the (meat) market square, this garden.

Only here he was. *He*, of all people! In this waystation? What a struggle it had been to step over the threshold. He remembers that first time. Thinking:

Everyone's staring
everyone's gesturing
everyone's hissing
everyone is laughing
everyone everyone everyone

Only there was no "everyone." Just an occasional inscrutable glance. And then later, smiles from the regulars. Once even, a wink from a god. The slip of a boy who had once sat in the front, completed homework worthy of gold star, stayed late in the hopes of avoiding the jeers and the punches in the shadows of corridors, the schoolyard, and streets, and who now hoped to avoid new jeers and punches with his updated figure, was being rewarded for his effort, for his persistence. He was, wasn't he?

Only when he was back home beneath a god who had somehow not looked away, who had said "I like your orange glasses" as he walked with him from the garden into the inner and outer sanctums of ecstasy, when he was reveling in this mass that undulated over and into him, he detected a faint sound. A rustling it was. In the corner? No, beyond. In the bedroom closet? Further still. In (or near) the proverbial closet? A cream muslin frock was whispering in the wind. He could hear the breeze separating its folds. There was a red-and-white gingham picnic blanket beneath, which only heightened the plain resplendence of its skirts. And there was a stroll between birches, and he could see the frock gleaming between the whites of the trunks, and he could hear the frock murmuring, calling, insisting to him.

Only the frock's lilt never did leave him. Rather, its notes escorted him as he returned to the dungeon, to the comrades-in-lifting, where the conductor of that earlier ecstasy was no longer to be found. Notes of what-might-have-been. Trills, thrills of what might yet be. Where would the frock apparition lead him? Could he follow it to its exquisite, terrifying confusion ... I mean, conclusion? As he made his way through the clang of iron and later into to the baths of anti-purification, he felt the frock's fabric caress the (hard-earned!) swell of his ass, then flutter off beyond his reach, beyond the bodies flashing in locker room gloaming.

Stasis at the Interstices

Maybe you'll grow to love your beard, *they* said, doubt hovering all around, then converging on a red dot moving behind his head. Think: thick ash blond waves. Envision: distinguished. Relax: Just let biology be destiny. The *they* shifted from time to time. Friends. Doctors. Manscapers. Mostly, *they* were just voices indeterminate. Concerned. External, internal, often. To escape them, he had to look elsewhere. Anywhere, really.

Lo tasuru ahare levavhem ve-ahare eneyekhem/Turn not after your heart and after your eyes. After, or rather, toward, the television show with the duo—no, the duet—of the highway cops in the tightly-fitting uniforms that he would watch regularly, desperately, on the filth box, when Sister and he snuck up to Great-Aunt's third floor apartment when she lived in their house. *Is Sister seeing what I am seeing? Is she watching me watch what I should not be watching/what she herself is watching?* And toward the magazines that he'd buy from the news kiosks on Chestnut Street to pore over the glistening physiques, the impassive faces, sculpted, the bodies he longed for and tried so hard in vain to emulate. The off-centerfolds.

But the looking wasn't enough. How could it be? If he only looked like this, then … *you would see me.* Then, he would move from consumer to consumed. Then he could be loved. Only his efforts to replicate, or even approximate, those physiques proved largely fruitless, if not failed outright.

But mostly the voices emerged from, were lodged in, the distant, the rear internal. Rattling around but not upsetting the cobwebs. Then settling there, "setting up shop." Except there was nothing to buy. It was all free for the taking. Have at it. Dysmorphia and dysphoria for sale! Two for one. A bargain. For he never did quite come to love his beard. Neither the one of face nor the one of body.

Instead, he imagined his body without hair at all, a smooth blank canvas on which to project another self. An other, yes. He had to imagine. For Nair was no option, leaving only trails of red dots. Furious were those follicles. Why shouldn't they be? The hairs hadn't asked to be nuked. I mean, Nair'ed. Was this what it meant to be in between? Okay, fine. Well, back to the beard then. Comb it. Curl it. Wave it. Brush it. Groom it.

Me? You—yes, you. So what if you've never been a groom? Or a bride? Your mother could not be/was never here to accompany you down the aisle in white satin with a seed pearl-encrusted bodice and orange blossoms in your hair. The lustrous curls. The beardlessness. Yet you still heard her whisper that you looked radiant in white on this sacred day. That she had never seen you quite so. That she was so proud that you had made it here. Beneath the intricate lace veil, you could still see the tremulous flame of the candle she held in her right hand. And of course, you could feel the crook of her arm guide you down the aisle toward the canopy that never was. The road out of here. The plate that was never smashed. The occasion to invoke the sorrow over the destruction of the Temple of Jerusalem in a moment of joy and celebration never materialized. The aisle never was.

Still, even if not a wedding gown, there are so many options here. Dresses. Skirts. Why not? You used to. And yes, Sister was pleased back then. So long ago. The time before beard. B.B., may we say? Sister understood, wanted you to be who you are. Loved to have you to try "stuff" on. Silky this-and-nylon that's that she couldn't, or at least, didn't want to put on. Pull off. There were things to be found in thrift shops. Such as silver, high-heeled shoes to clonk around in. Costume apparel. Paste jewelry. See how that glass daisy catches the glint in the tower. That cameo brooch suits you. And so does this *sheytl*, this wig. The third floor was far away. Safe.

But the child's playroom can migrate. It's portable. The foundation is mighty. Dress up, dress down. Robes, at least. Muumuus? Housecoats then. Yes, silk flowered housecoats shimmering in the private sphere. Skorts? No, no, never those! Well, if you don't come to love the beard, then use make-up. You've seen the competitions, the races and so on. The transformations. You don't have to choose. You can be both. You can be more. You can be all. You can be none. Muscle Mary. "Artsy" Arnold. Two-spirit, three-spirit. Or more. You know what to do. No excuse. Not today. Plunge into the pool. Mind the chlorine. Take care with the prescriptions. Careful with the chemicals. Maybe you'll finally learn to swim.

Portamento, Prayer

The waters will not engulf you.

How could they?
Such blue, such aquamarine. Pool Placid.
Without the threat of tides, waves, tidal waves.

The pool boy—no, pool man—was here.
Yesterday.
I saw you sneaking a peek. Some peeks.

These mosaics in the shapes of waves,
catch rays glinting as they never can
in the subway stations of 59th Street

and Christopher Street where once you sashayed in pristine liberation
garlanded in colossal pink beads and a pink triangle
a pilgrimage to the holy site   that holy street

after which was named a reader, a chrestomathy,
articles pooled from the magazines
an anthology acquired even earlier from Giovanni's chamber

whose pages you fingered
treasured
in your boyhood garret

even if you never quite made it to the inner sanctum
or any sanctum at all
always outside looking in

the movement advocate in
and out of the movement
mostly out   in deed at least

the dream of the collective honed
the tyrant toppled   strong man no longer
his statue clattering down in the town square of power

the price of medication lowered
the river scoured
the air oh the air

no more orange air
no more we say
a blue sky shall not be a rarity.

may the water not engulf you
may your father's hands
that tossed you into the swimming pool

when you were little
be a memory bleached   or at least no longer so neon
a mythos no longer

may his hands guide you through water's embrace
water love father son
water

may you glide with his guidance
separate from the drumbeat of that paternal requirement in the Talmud
Glissando

from here to there
from little one to adult
may there be no tsunami

as you walk by ocean edge
for you will not stand a chance
with the peaches rotting from

the neon of those hands
your failure to relinquish
their grip around your five-year old frame

may our houses
not be engulfed
reduced to wreckage

or to green and black and shade indeterminate
so different from this aquamarine
with nothing to salvage

may these notes not be connected
may your body be caressed by this slosh so gentle
hugged by mosaic waves still glinting

may these waters be clear
and free of plastic and pesticide
and full yes of purity

may these waters not engulf you

The Babe's Legacy

Once, Father played catch with me.
I watched his athletic frame move with grace.
Transfixed.
At one with the grass and the afternoon,
as if he were on a diamond and there were throngs cheering.

Without his kapote, there was such an easy physicality to him,
despite the years buried in the ruminations of the rabbis.
His massive hand gripped the ball, knowing when to let go.
Two skills I have never mastered.
Knowing how to grip a baseball and knowing when to let go.

He raised his left leg,
as if his body were steeped in the muscle memory of pitching.
I remembered the stories,
how little boy Father had somehow snuck into Yankee Stadium,
past a guard or a turnstile or a gap in some fence.

All this to witness the glory of the Babe, who did not disappoint.
Two home runs witnessed by the young future lecturer on rabbinical
literature.
To be a part of throngs who really were cheering.
What was the path of that boy to this father?
This paterfamilias now pitching with such poise.

Now we were a part of the national tradition.
Even if we never celebrated Thanksgiving.
Even if the Gentiles threw rotten eggs and tomatoes at us
when we walked by.
Or hissed. Or threw pennies.

Or called us names.
Here, we were,
like any father and son rooted
in an ancient ritual in a small yard on a broad continent.
We belonged in this country. Didn't we?

So caught was I in these ruminations
that I missed the ball sailing from him.

Lobbed by him, really.
For Father knew,
as much as he didn't want to know.

Word would have gotten back to him.
How my schoolmates picked me last,
not always cheerfully bearing the burden of me.
There was no one who didn't know,
even if no one had to directly report it to him.

And as the ball plopped onto the ground right next to me,
as if without warning, or preamble of any kind,
Father shouted words of encouragement.
Don't worry. Today, there are no worries.
Don't give up.

I "threw" it back to him.
Only it didn't land anywhere near him.
And still Father would not be deterred.
So it went. On and on for the rest of that day.
For the rest of time.

Finally, Father said it was time to call it a day,
And what a day it had been. A day never to be repeated.
A day never recorded in a familial or communal register,
but still one for the books.
The history books. Or the poetry ones.

His voice was light,
but disappointment had accumulated,
was now etched
in the lines around his eyes,
the misery in his mighty shoulders.

Crash Course in the Classics

He returned to his teacher. Somewhere in a far-flung corner of the virtual realm he had located her. Forays in the then new world. Just write. So he did. Just call, she said. So he did. His fingers didn't tremble. He was in control. The self was surely assured. Suddenly, her voice. It hadn't changed. The warmth of the drawl. The welcome of its extended sounds. Magically, he was thirteen again, immersed in her lectures on the Peloponnesian War. On Sparta and Carthage. There he was on the beaches of Mykonos.

And the diagramming of sentences; the precision of the language whose mysteries she uncovered for him. Or guided his discovery of. An infectious love. And lo, he who was always picked last for baseball or soccer or basketball or volleyball; he who stumbled in the labyrinth of the Talmud; he who forgot which blessing to recite on noodle kugel and tomatoes and buckwheat and pizza found a place for himself. Saw a way forward. The marble statues made room for him in their halo. He caressed the muscular deities. The man gods. The god-men. He turned to worship them. He would be their servant. Gladly would he serve. And his teacher gasped at his ravenousness, fed him more. Read this. Tell me what you perceive. She marveled at his embrace of the Hellenists, his fluid paeans to their celebration of wisdom and debauchery. And her praise, her attention, set him on the path. To this book-lined garret.

And he told of what he'd been reading since those long-ago sojourns in the realms of the deities. Of interests in a more recent old language, sometimes said to be in a renaissance of its own. Sometimes said to now be the new Latin or Ancient Greek, popping up in academe, yet now with (comparatively) few native speakers. A language that beckoned a bridge back to his own tradition. Then, she spoke of her children and her return to the ancestral home high in the mountains and of grand-children and new pupils who themselves were reading. Devouring. She asked him about children of his own or a significant other. And he said there were none. Was none. And he could have left it at that, evaded as he so often did; using an ambiguous pronoun or avoiding one altogether. Instead, he just blurted it out. The unspeakable vice of the Greeks. His interest wasn't academic. Well, not just academic. Had never been.

And he felt the floor give way, saw the chasm open between them. The silence wailed. The darkness burned. Aargh! You … goose! Why did you have to…? What a cozy reunion they had been fashioning … and now this.

And suddenly excuses were proffered. Something about the grandchildren and reading time. The dog needing walking. Then, click. She was gone. He held the handset until the dial tone returned, and then the beeps. He disregarded their urgency. He left it off its cradle for days. Then weeks.

Perhaps if I had traveled to see her, he thought much later. If I had crossed multiple state lines on the train, trees flitting by. The canopy of green might have fortified me. I might have interacted with the grandchildren or the dog. I could have read the visual cues. I could have revealed without revealing. I could have enabled textual exegesis of myself. I would have had to be seen. It might have gone differently. The chasm might have been smaller, or not as visible. I might have returned to this book-lined garret with cherry blossoms garlanded around my shaved skull. Without ashes rising into my throat.

Ardor in and out of the Catacombs

During the hours of the sun, she worked behind the counter and among the shelves. Only the sun never reached her or her charges who had to be safeguarded from the devastation of its rays. If she'd been permitted, she would have worn a hat with an awning of a brim, not to shield her pallor from that orb aforementioned, not to be fashionable, not to make a statement of some kind, but to deflect attention: the side-eyed scorn, the glowers. If only I could be invisible, she thought. She understood what a visitor—an interloper—was really asking: the goal behind the question, the Eden vibrating beneath the paltry articulated. That goal, that Eden, was there, waiting to be excavated, she would tell her interns.

But she herself was happiest when she was away from the questions, far from the oily hands grasping for, groping these photographs, those pages. From the eyes. Even with the many regulations, she feared for her charges' safety, for their longevity. She was happiest in the frigid, windowless catacombs, where she could whisper and hum and listen and coax documents into protective covering that would ensure their enduring beyond her. The crackle of envelopes, folders, and boxes seemingly so banal could never diminish the splendor of her slog. Of that she was certain.

She understood systems of knowledge organization: where to place things and why. Without proper placement, an item is gone to the generations. The key to ending disease or genocide might be lost a mile of a folder or box away or at least until randomly uncovered by an underling, a youngster who hadn't quite absorbed the scope and urgency of her doctrine, who perhaps had been solving a calculus problem or thinking about the best pizza in town or cheerleader practice or why Jimmy still hadn't called while she was expounding—*compellingly* she had hoped—on those very systems of information organization. She thought she had an unfailing eye for discerning talent, kindred spirits. Only her eye was not infallible. Even she, anchored in the shrewdness of her ministration, could be misled.

Yet, for all her rigor during the hours of the sun, night was her milieu. For it was then that she took to her desk, where words of pleasure and cleaving came to her. She wrote freely, without anxiety, or consideration of condemnation. Here were contained images of the body, of bodies linking, some might say fornicating, in delight. Bodies of all shapes and sizes and colors. There was no angst or uncertainty or inadequacy. With her words, she had solved the flesh-spirit dilemma. Or rather skirted it altogether.

They were one, her delicate, fiery constellations maintained. Here was the unification, the love, that the philosophers and poets had been seeking all this time.

And her writings did find their way into the world. Yes, she did receive messages of admiration, adulation even, for she always wrote under her birth name. And so she was known, or rather, not at all known. For none could understand how such texts could have emerged from her, from such a … here, they resorted to animal comparisons—mouse-, frog-, horse-like—creature. How could her configuration of words, with their texture and carnality and specificity of experience, arise from someone who seemingly had none. Really, the audacity! How indeed, they wondered, as they whispered in the marketplace (prodding the cantaloupe) and tut-tutted at her latest offering, now well-worn, almost threadbare, as it was, after all, too delicious, too terrible, not to be shared.

And thus, the mystery of her remained, for no one could bring themselves to ask her. They didn't dare. It wouldn't be right to the poor thing. And perhaps, too, they preferred not to know. As it is said: Some things are best left unsaid. Yet when they glimpsed her departing the temple of learning, when they beheld her lack of response to the carpenter's "Good morning," when they decided not to tell her that it wouldn't hurt her to smile or say "Good morning" back now would it, when they found their usual pity for her strangely misplaced, or even absent altogether, they couldn't help but marvel at her devotion to a life of the mind *and* of the flesh, for her elegant insistence on their inseparability. Fleetingly, they imagined that only she had the answer to the essential riddle of existence, that only she truly *understood* (they weren't exactly sure of what), that she must be a witch or a prophetess or, at the very least, a high priestess of the night.

And they decided that it was time to get ready for dinner. Yes, it was high time. And as they served the brisket and string beans and mashed potatoes laced with garlic, they wondered what she was ingesting, what fleshly delights she was conjuring and when they would get to devour them. And, too, whether the moon would soon illuminate her pale figure beneath a garret skylight as she slipped beneath the heirloom quilt and into the embrace of the silver nocturne.

City of Sweets

The bells tolled at dusk and into starlight
indifferent to the breezes of unease poking at serenity's edge

Still the ice cream parlor with its pink and turquoise sundae sign swaying
above the door   on whose benches lovebirds swore eternal devotion

was open
and the bakery with its confections and concoctions

was not without its own steady stream of devotees the commuters
stopping by after work for sweetmeat for sweetheart or sweet pea

or to wolf down a cheese donut or plum dumpling in secret
and with the stockpiling of milk blinking on the outskirts of rumor

we didn't allow ourselves to think about how much longer this vanilla
and raspberry and Dobos torte decadence would stay available

And still I walked along the paths of the municipal garden
spectacularly groomed on the we might as well say the eve of the
          apocalypse

farther and farther past the evergreen and the briefly red and white
though time was hardly crawling toward curfew

and Mama would be writhing and wringing and practically weeping
          with worry
I could see her pacing hear the floorboards creaking underneath

though I had told her not to
as I was only stepping out for an evening constitutional

And then I was there in the forest of the city's beyond
where I was sometimes called when mother's fret was too much to bear

and I came upon you not expecting you but still hoping for you
and suddenly I was surrounded by you

and you did not mind
even seemed to rejoice in

my concave chest spindly legs the unvoluptuousness of my ass
the density of these spectacles formed for the caressing of pages

only some of the shortcomings as the not-friends had long ago labeled them
that I had so endeavored in vain to undo

and my arms encircled your strength that kept the curfew
and the students' papers yet to be graded at bay

and I could not believe it was you
and I dropped to my knees in gratitude and adoration

and then when you when we were spent
you kissed me unbidden and fondled Mama's worry

etched into my body and eyes
and later I saw the metal buttons of your uniform

winking back at me as you waved to me
as you smiled to me now from afar

telling me that this once
on this one and only ever night

with the bells tolling
the ice cream parlor and bakery as yet unshuttered

the breezes of unease subtly but surely turning into winds
I might could possibly   yes even if only this once   be luminous

Village Tableau, Far From the Parade

The emptiness within the gilded frame faces me.
Confronts me.

The pendulum of someone's lovingly-polished grandfather clock
swings back and forth in the hallway. Its horses will not be held.

Not exactly a tick-tock, but still a two-sided sound.
Yin and yang of Mother Time.

And the hallway floors devoid of runner of any kind are polished, too.
Mother T.'s younger sister Auntie Beulah sees to that.

Her hands gnarled, resplendent. Deft with the polish rag
and plaits of all kinds. Hair. Lanyard. Yarn.

How to weave the yarns, these other yarns,
match the variegated threads.

Would to say by saying,
tell with telling.

This tongue not shuttered,
but clipped, fettered.

Oh, this obliqueness.
Aargh to this between-the-line-ness.

Is that my body staring back at me from the void?
Is a picture needed here?

One in which I'm placing one foot before the other,
the clicking of my heels echoing over the cobblestones beyond the frame.

Only I hear other footsteps behind me.
Heavy ones.

And I know I'm not imagining a helmet gleaming above
and a night stick restless at the side.

Thud thud. Clomp clomp.
Or is it thud clomp, thud clomp?

Surely, these steps would have tired of me by now.
Surely, I could have stared their owners down,

invited them into the peal and guffaw and clink and souse
open until late beyond last call,

found a way to lose them in this labyrinth of alleys
for which our village is so renowned.

Come, all ye lost souls!
Lose and find yourselves over these cobblestones.

Surely, I could find a way to elude
the barbed-wire enclosures that had once been

and no longer are but might yet still …
I hate to say, to name, what.

Surely, the ducking, this skirting, can be behind me.
Auntie Beulah won't let me fall.

All these years,
and still this hiding.

Polemic on Pallor and Parchment

Sometimes the words are loath to cleave to course
even if there are more than enough of them
careening in and out of the cupboard of mind
opinions three-quarters baked in reaction to this or that verbiage
metastasizing from the headline or post or billboard or broadside or flyer
doomsnight scroll before and between fitful slumber
against the counsel of all the sleep specialists

Sometimes the words cannot escape the impossibility
of the horror they aim to capture
the dire calamity of the moment fluorescent
this blood-drenched hour
the dragging from bed   the seizure of self from safety
the beheading broadcast
the intimacy of atrocity what Goya pictured

Sometimes the words cannot be summoned
for it is the images that flit dart predominate in tones of gray and sepia
the ones longed etched into our bones' eye
running whirring rattling on the loop of history's sledgehammer
the doors smashed down   the glass shattered the bodies strewn
        in the street
the breath held in the crawlspace where a smudge of dust is the
        only telltale sign
the bloodhounds baying in the forest sniffing for terror or a doll's bisque
        head

Sometimes the words cannot be borne
why are you not here   why were you not there
        why did you not come
how dare you speak from your far-away your not-knowing
from your comfort in the stone house set in rolling fields glib with
        goldenrod
horses grazing in contentment goats bleating in merriment
the moors of your complacency the quagmire of armchair commentary
what know you of this agony

Sometimes sometimes
and yet sometimes   words
bring us to and, even if with averted eyes, across from each other
dampen the cannon's fire   blunt the sword's tip
help us imagine black bread and rhubarb preserves in the larder
Leah in a silk wedding gown trimmed with orange blossoms
Nona with the medicine she needs to remain and recount her recipes and
          yarns

Sometimes there are words that cannot be ignored unheeded
perhaps you will hear the tendrils of your neighbors' gossip
in the noonday courtyard beneath your window
          or the young man
setting his bike against the bricks calling out "Delivery!"
or the life saved by lullaby and chamomile
and your beloved brother refusing to leave your fevered side
and you will rise from the dusk of indeterminacy

And you who are chortling in the back of the room
gazing with a skeptical then mocking eye at this earnestness
you who insist on the supremacy of touch gesture   action
and you who have been unable to emerge from beneath the eiderdown will
forge a way back to words will know there is no other way for wordlessness
though vital cannot be eternal
and words too can glow in groves of hush

so come
if not to embrace or celebrate
then to inhabit this shortcoming
come
to create these other sometimes-es of prospect
into this parchment vase
come arrange these snapdragons of solace

Activist's Retreat

Today, I will not watch the news. I will not listen to the radio. I will not browse or descend into my doomscroll. I deliver this staccato not as declaration, but as aspiration, goal posts jitterbugging in my haze-daze of blue. Markers of a possible world. Fireflies flickering in the dread of democracy's dusk. I will have the good fortune, the luxury of so doing … for now, at least. This garret is not under attack. The invaders aren't (yet) here, although their emissaries have been active. And who knows when… So yes, the luxury of turning off. Tuning out.

For so many do not have such a luxury. Cannot afford to. What with the bombs dropping everywhere. With supply lines being cut off. With the invaders coming so you must run to find shelter, to escape. Only to where? On one moonless night you dreamed of flying away on the iridescent wings of a drone. Crone on a drone. Only you must find food. Remember the chicken couscous you once spent hours getting just so? Remember the date treats—how no oven was needed? And the baklava… Is that rose water you smell in the smolder? Remember the burgundy damask settee in the once-parlor where you received the luminaries of the streets? Now is not the time to remember. Yesterday, you thought you saw a shredded patch of that damask caught between the rocks and the smithereens of your once-neighborhood. But when you reached for it, it was gone. There has to be a way of getting water. A working toilet, if not toilet paper. Insulin? You've heard J has a connection. Avoid that road—what's left of it—they say it's littered with landmines.

Today, I will not make a donation. I will not drum up support. I will not sign the petition. I will not knock on doors. Not write to my congressperson. Not attend this meeting. Yes, I organized it, but I never promised I'd go. S can chair it. It'll be in good hands, you'll see. I've written the agenda. P can take the minutes. The essential labor of those far from cataclysm. Who will cauterize as they can. With talking. Giving and taking. Hopefully, more giving than taking. Today, I will not inveigh against the news that is not the enemy of the people, even if it could do more for the people. The heads talking. The sets gleaming. The ideas that ought to have been aired.

Today, I will not embark on an excursion into the forest. I will not go on a hike to the peak where the convergence of three states can be seen. I will not walk along the water's edge, wondering when the steel heavens will burst, when the waters from above and below will link. Today, I will not play with my neighbor's beagle, frolicking with him in the park. I will not fly a kite, revel in red and yellow soaring into blue. I will not make pumpkin pie, even though the day would surely benefit from it, from spices suffusing the stratosphere. Yes, there can be cinnamon again someday.

Today, I will not constructively clean the dust clotting the pages of my anti-imperialist tomes. I will not speak to the solutions that I won't be offering. Or the action I won't take. I won't speak of restoration or rejuvenation. Or lessons learned. I won't comment on the tangled tango of my privilege.

Today, I will not...

Today, instead, I will lower my eyelids. I will be still. I will reach into leafy. I will sit on the straw floor mat. Only occasionally will I move. I will be aware of but apart from my advantages. Even if only for the duration of this extended moment. I will listen to the bells in my ears that never cease tolling. Resisting ragged, I will heed my breath—air entering and leaving. Call and response. Call, pause, and response. Light through and through the whoosh of the whisper of waves. Within. I will feel the time it takes. Or rather, my skin will. Sometimes the cycles will change shape and size and color. Yes, there will be lavender cycles. And ones in that old favorite: seafoam. There are bound to be. Chest rising and falling. The miracle of God's movement. Or what others call... Only the neighbor will observe the noiselessness of my stance. Only later will I realize that she muted her radio, source of news of the relatives who couldn't get out, of her only son ensnared in Armageddon's net. Only the yellow eye slits, the twitching ears of her black cat seated next to the potted geranium on the fire escape ledge will detect the creep of shadows around the lotus position of my oblivion.

Today, I will not.... *Only today.*

Tomorrow, I will return to...

Mirage No. 2

And I am over the moon with this new sun
that peers warily then evenly in response to September rain

into which the gods had led me following words exchanged
and which emblazoned the meadows with a violet hitherto unseen

I did not expect this light
did not seek it in fact fled from it

craving the forgiveness of shadow and stone wall
across which moss spread and ivy clung threatening to choke

only here now is this frolic across hearth
an embrace of harvest amassed from the inferno of Hades' dominion

an agility of beam meandering and knitting
so that once gray and brown is now fleetingly sparkle

in this scrounged room this interval pilfered
for lo seven years I must not tarry in the damp and chill

and here by this platform startlingly bejeweled
wrought of centuries' patience and sudden sweat and thwack

with its roses daubed by Gran's then-steady hand
and exhortations to humility overhead and columns supple alongside

all that I had asked for which I presumed to be miniscule
is brought forth from mineral   is conferred

and those words exchanged though not retracted nor redeemed
are backgrounded

and there is your touch upon the stoop that is my shoulder
not leading me but being with me in this room transformed into chamber

and there can now be no question of the chamber's aftermath
of diplomacy that may stumble beyond this hearth dance

and I am over the moon with this old sun
And I am suffused in smolder in the foresight of that September rain

Permanent Resident, Without Green Card

You could find yourself a room. Elsewhere. Far from or close to here. In a respectable house. Furnished. Small, well-appointed. A bed. A desk. A small icebox. Madam Sunderlin sees to the comfort of all of her "guests." There would be meals shared or brought to your room. There, you might consider in moonlight our once-bounty. The choreography of our days, our decades that followed the jubilation of our foundational canopy evening, the ambiguity of our nuptial night. The ways in which banality can glow when left unrecited. What we were. Creations matched long ago, forged in the benediction of the Divine, in the formulas and diagrams of Kabbalah. And you might consider what you want now. What will be available to you now. For your options will be diminished. Word will have gotten out. Without my having seen to that. The moon's light will generate insight if you remain open to the pallor of its beams, to the determination in their progress. If insight isn't thus generated, don't blame the moon. Or the stars, for that matter. Look within. Or you could spread out your favorite volumes of verse on the spindly yet strangely sturdy writing desk. Perhaps even pen some of your own, again, that is, if you are at ease with the moon. It's all a question of synchronicity so don't blather on about the "block" that has plagued you and your ilk. I won't be there to hear it, in any case. Nor will anyone else. You could stroll the small square several blocks from the house, with its tidy paths, box hedges, spruces, where the stone angel spreads her wings of magnanimity over all who cross her path and even those who don't, where others similarly or dissimilarly situated sometimes linger into the night. You all know how to be seen and not seen in the streetlights' radiance. Since you cannot bring them to your own room, you may even dare to go home with one or more of them in carefully timed intervals or in sudden bursts of hunger and audacity. Remember, the more you engage, the more risk you incur. They may be repelled by the perfume of me, by the stench of your rebuff—no, your abandonment—of me still hovering on your jacket collar. For yes, it was abandonment, although you may call it self-discovery, the discovery, finally, of your true self. Or you may convince them to hold their nose, tantalize them with some sort of reward. The promise of ... well ... whatever little it is that you can promise. You may find fleeting reprieve in their hard, indifferent thrusts, in a room you might otherwise never have found yourself had you not trashed the prescience of the Zohar. Perhaps overlooking the docks. Or the pencil factories. Or the slaughterhouses. No matter. When you leave, when you're back in your room, I will be there, too. I won't go into what I will do. I haven't decided yet. But I will be there, too. The anguish of my nights will ravage your resources for rest. The white knuckles of my rage will silence the siren song of sleep.

Glass Dreams

In dream,
my father witnessed the ceremonial conclusion
of my apprentice scholar period—
when my name was summoned into awakening—
accepts my absence from the quorum of gents,
recognizes my alternative Sabbath days,
beams with pride at my harvest,
recites selections from the lyrics, even the bawdy ones,
encourages me to go a courting, to welcome Prince Charming—
with his as yet undefined salt-and-pepper-beard,
now astride a recalcitrant mule,
now walking along a desolate country road,
now bent over a baroque farce winking in fuchsia omniscience—
delights in my flavors,
the ways of me,
my rare bird perched against a stunned sunset on the fire escape ledge.

In dream,
my mother survived
the surge of sugar,
the waves of discord
crashing both upstairs and down,
the scarcity of bloom and caress,
the long-night interlude rigid in the bed of turbulence,
aghast against the adamant prohibitions,
the flight from Sabbath feast
somehow conjured onto wan cloth,
the anguish over the nearly born,
the invasion of tumor,
the varicose veins,
all the lost years,
the heart not shuttered,
but worn down.

In dream,
we are a family on rain-soaked terra firma.
Zevulun wants to know how I resolved a thorny translation matter.
I inquire after his mastery of the sacred slang
blended in the kosher dairy fast-foodery.

Rinah beckons me,
not for a candlelit Sabbath,
but for leftover potato kugel
and chocolate peanut butter squares and almond milk,
better that we may banter
without partition, without veil, without ritual,
reunite for intermezzo, however occasional,
put down our walking sticks
to gather bluebells and buttercups and black-eyed Susans,
to reminisce with fondness
on (imagined) Augusts by the lake of long ago.

Upon awakening,
I handle the items on this impossible (dirty) laundry list—
these dreams—
with tenderness, however wary; with regard, however prickly.
I place them gingerly in the curio cabinet behind the kitchen table.
There, they sparkle in the fury of the obscure sun of noonday,
gleam in the glow of moon and stars and comets.
And yes, in the blue of constellations, too.
From time to time, in their relentless ingenuity,
in their vinegar resolve,
they escape the locked doors—
all the futile precautions—
and pirouette and skip about my garret quarters.
Somehow, I manage to capture them,
though they have darted from my grip,
and return them to their place of Sabbath unrest.

Night of Seroconversion and Aftermath/Dialogue, in Eternal Embryo

I.

Was it good that night
   did you meet him
in a bar
or on the street
or in the bathhouse
or along the piers
   did the stars sparkle   reassure   prod
against an aghast blue-black sky

were there shadows as witness
   flitting in   and out of   your lines of sight
did his return gaze lure you
   in spurts of beckoning
or in a single line of insistence
was your heart pounding in anxiety and thrill or
   did you know that this was your destiny
that this needed to happen

did you go into the brambles
   or onto a rooftop
or into an alley
or between two diner trash bins
or a hotel room
or an apartment tidy but impervious
   with two nightlights moaning
back at you in the gray-gold gloom

did you at first sink to your knees in delight
   to ready him
to ready you
   to ready the night itself
or did you bend over right away
the idea of protection flitting
   then vanishing out of reach   gone
banished by your hunger or his impatience   or

did you think to inquire about his status
    or was that not even an option in the urgency of desire
was his entry gentle but insistent
or indifferent determined or
was it glorious or   ordinary and adequate
did you assemble a rhythm in unison
    were your bodies rowing
climbing through and towards the eye of fire

did he and you last long
    or was it over all too soon
crumbs of carnality
post-deluge puddles evanescent below the desert sun
    or the city moon
did he say beforehand
    that he was going to pull out
or was that never mentioned   whispered

did he kiss   embrace   you goodbye
    or nod so that only his teeth sparkled at you
did his face appear before you when
    your hands grazed mine in the "cinema"
in the so many nights later that followed
    when our lips strained
        and our torsos trembled
in the face of such exhilaration

until they (sort of) went their separate ways
    would you have stayed with me
(longer)
if I had asked these questions
if I had been able to formulate them
without audacity
    with care
if I had bent over in abandon

II.

Do you think you can ask such questions
do you think you have a right to know
what right
what business is it of yours
you who have never surrendered to glory   not really
never   abandoned yourself to it
            do you think you've ever escaped
the "puritanism" of your upbringing

have you ever turned your back on the rules
            do you understand the necessity of risk
the thrill the urgency of placing yourself in the path of peril
that through danger comes the glimpsing of
            the cleaving to
                        the Divine
does it matter where that coming together happened
is this a play or a novel with a declared setting

or is only the night unmoored writ large the setting
would it please you
            if I told you I feared the arrival of the police
do your questions ever escape the taint of voyeurism
            do they move you into participant
                        do you relish the role of judge
black robes swishing beneath fluorescent light
or   schoolmaster tsk-tsk-ing at me

do you think that if he had entered in latex
then my love of self would be deep   "authentic"   true
                        healthy
if he had known me beforehand
if we had initially chit-chatted about off-Broadway offerings in a café
                        would I have been less hungry
less condemnable
            more worthy of

do you think your body is more sacred
                    do you think you are cleaner than I
how could there be room for me and my
          what with that stick stuck up your
do you think that   that night is worthy of this scrutiny
when all that matters is the drive toward eros   toward joy
          why should Thanatos have the upper hand
is there safety in shelter in the circumspect   avoidance of life

when you were with me
                    what were you protecting yourself from
did you ever see me
          was I ever more than a vessel of restraint trashed
          of acumen abandoned
when we were together
          did you ever stop summoning him
          your imagined monster of carelessness

stud of blue-black night
did you ever let us breathe into black dahlias
did you ever stop condemning me
for refusing to discard that night
for refusing   for stepping away
from the cold handcuffs
                    the implacability
          of your court sentencing

Rendezvous Fantasia

Here you are, after all these years.
You've chosen our diner.
Well done.
It's still open,
and our favorite waitress still works here,
although, despite her politeness,
it's clear she doesn't remember us.
I order the Cobb salad (minus the bacon),
and you the turkey burger.
I find comfort in ritual so abruptly restored
and resilience in this linoleum terra firma.

Here you are, after all these years,
Time has not been genteel.
We're both heavier than we were,
than we ought to be. Our hair has turned
to shades of pollution and slush.
Yours once shone strawberry and carrot.
There are lines where once smoothness reigned,
sagging where once tautness,
trepidation where once ease.
Still, we savor the hearty fare,
the bonhomie of the unchanged neon.

Here you are, after all these years.
But your style still blossoms casual, elegant.
I like your charcoal gray sweater and burgundy shirt.
You were always so put together.
As always, you have arresting reading material.
Lately, you've been immersed in the essays of Montaigne.
The observations, the witty dissection of self
have never been more alluring. And the way you look at me,
into me—all I can do is look down. *Michel would get it!*
Your confidence has never been more polished.
Yes, pass the pepper please. Cheers.

Here you are, after all these years.
We never could find a way to be together.
You, managing the plague, plagued by a wandering eye,
and of late, the tangle of pills, powder, and needles.
I, with the dragons.
We tried so many different iterations:
lover, friend, reader, host.
Only always was the jangle beneath:
the accusations, the appraisals, the never-enough.
All of it is on hand, even today. But still this banter,
blessed by the waitress we are sure almost remembers us.

Cobb salad and turkey burger gone
(but not forgotten),
my hand on the door,
my body poised
between
kiss,
hug,
and handshake,
I wonder if this encounter actually happened
or whether it was a fantasy within a fantasy
and if there is a footpath out from anomaly.

Where to from these fluorescent lights?

My love, please don't die without me.

אָט ביסטו, נאָך די אַלע יאָרן.
מיר האָבן קיין מאָל ניט געקענט געפֿינען אַן אופֿן צו זײַן צוזאַמען.
דו, זיך ספראַווענדיק מיט דער פלאָג, געפלאָגט פון אַן אויג אַ וואַנדערן,
און לעצטנס, דעם פלאָנטער פון פראָשקעס, נאָדלען און פילן.
איך, מיט די דראַקאָנען.
מיר האָבן אויסגעפּרוּווט אַזוי פֿיל איטעראַציעס:
געליבטע, פֿרײַנד, לייענער, מכניס-אורחים.
אָבער שטענדיק דאָס קלימפּערײַ פֿון אונטן:
די באַשולדיקונגען, די אָפּשאַצונגען, די קיין-מאָל-ניט-גענוגען.
עס איז נמצא נאָך הײַנט. אָבער נאָך אַלץ דאָס פּלודערײַ,
געבענשט פֿון דער סאַרווערין וואָס געדענקט אונדז זיכער כּמעט.

קאַב-סאַלאַט און אינדיק-בורגער שוין ניטאָ
(אָבער ניט פֿאַרגעסן),
די האַנט אויף דער טיר,
דער גוף האַלט זיך
צווישן
קוש,
אַרומנעם,
און געבן זיך די הענט,
ווּנדער איך זיך צי די טרעפֿונג איז טאַקע געשען
צי איז עס געווען אַ פֿאַנטאַזיע אינעווייניק אַ פֿאַנטאַזיע
און צי געפֿינט זיך אַ סטעזשקע אַרויס פֿון דער אַנאָמאַליע.

אַוועק פֿון די פֿלואָרעסצענטע-ליכט, ווּהין?

קרוין מײַנער, ביטע שטאַרב ניט אָן מיר.

ראַנדעווו פֿאַנטאַזיע

אָט ביסטו, נאָך די אַלע יאָרן.
דו האָסט אויסגעקליבן דעם דײַנער.
גוט געטאָן.
ס'איז נאָך אַלץ אָפֿן,
און אונדזער באַליבסטע סאַרווערין אַרבעט נאָך אַלץ דאָ,
כאָטש, ניט געקוקט אויף איר העפֿלעכקייט,
איז עס קלאָר זי געדענקט אונדז ניט.
כ'באַשטעל דעם קאַב-סאַלאַט (אָן דעם בייקאָן),
און דו דעם אינדיק-בורגער.
כ'טרייסט זיך מיטן ריטואַל אַזוי פֿלוצעמדיק צוריקגעשטעלט
און געפֿין עלאַסטישקייט אין דער לינאָלייענער יבשה.

אָט ביסטו, נאָך די אַלע יאָרן.
די צײַט איז ניט געווען איידל.
מיר זײַנען ביידע דיקער ווי מיר זײַנען פֿריער געווען,
ווי מיר וואָלטן געדאַרפֿט זײַן. די האָר האָט באַקומען פֿאַרבן
פֿון סליאַטע און פֿאַרפֿעסטיקונג.
דײַנע פֿלעגן שײַנען ווי טרוסקאַפֿקע און מער.
פֿאַראַן קנייטשן ווו ס'פֿלעגט הערשן גלאַטיקייט,
עס הענגט אַראָפּ ווו ס'פֿלעגט זײַן אָנגעצויגן,
דאָס פֿלאַטערניש ווו ס'פּסלעגט זײַן גרינג.
דאָך באַלעקן מיר זיך מיטן געשמאַקן עסן
און מיט דער גוטמוטיקייט פֿונעם נעאָן דעם ניט-געביטענעם.

אָט ביסטו, נאָך די אַלע יאָרן.
אָבער דײַן סטיל צעבליט זיך נאָך אומפֿאָרמעל, עלעגאַנט.
דײַן האָלצקויל-גרוי-סוועטער און ווײַן־רויט העמד געפֿעלן מיר.
ביסט אַלע מאָל אַזוי שיין אָנגעטאָן, "צונויפֿגעשטעלט."
ווי שטענדיק האָסטו פֿאַרכאַפֿנדיקע לייענוואַרג.
לעצטנס האָסטו זיך פֿאַרטיפֿט אין די עסייען פֿון מאָנטעניע.
די באַמערקונגען, דער קלוגער חשבון-הנפֿש
זיינען קיין מאָל ניט געווען מער צוציִענדיק. און ווי דו קוקסט אויף מיר,
אין מיר אַרײַן—ווי אַן ענטפֿער קען איך נאָר נידערן דעם בליק. *מישעל וואָלט פֿאַרשטאַנען!*
דײַן זיכצוטרוי איז קיין מאָל ניט געווען מער גלאַנצנדיק.
יאָ, דערלאַנג מיר ביטע דעם פֿעפֿער. אַ דאַנק.

Throne, with Cat

If I were in a thrift shop,
the backdrop would only heighten its charm.
Ah yes, there is the ancient prophetess who nudges me forward.
The specter of negotiation shall not be summoned.
The racks of polyester shirts and slim neckties and chiffon frocks
and Bakelite-buttoned hounds tooth coats,
the framed prints of rock stars once drooled over,
would all give way,
retreat to the bleachers.
Its ashes-of-rose folds would beckon,
brightening my day mild.

If I were in a museum,
it would sit atop a mini-dais.
A crystal decanter might sparkle just off to its right.
Only just in time would I withdraw my fingertips
from the mead residue particles I imagined there.
There would be a placard praising its form—
both voluptuous and spare—
clarifying its standing in the history of dazzle.
Against the whiteness of the walls
and the company of compatriots of earlier eras,
it would surely elicit admiration, however measured.

If I were in a shrine,
passersby might gawk,
drawn by flames flickering in weeping glass
and the relief of acceptable mourning.
Incense smoke might float upwards.
Flowers in various stages of decay might be visible.
In the gloom,
it will be hard to know for sure.
And even if deciphered,
it would be off limits,
as if cordoned off by a rope of my own twisting.

Only we are in this poem;
this is what's left to me.

Between these words,
the sun demarcates the disparity
between the auburn of your head locks
and the ginger of your beard.
You look up from trumpets blaring,
hips shimmying,
sopranos trilling,
cross your legs,
and smile at me.

The feral cat you rescued from the alley
writhes, restless beneath the glide of your hand,
unable to endure, unable to turn away from such pleasure.
Because I never shared her ambivalence,
I understand its utility, its necessity.
Somehow the cat knows not to scratch
those spindly-strong cherry wood legs.
I've never said a word to her.
There was never time.
She slinks in and out of your presence—
just as she does in this poem.

This poem might have been visualized in a well-appointed room.
The secret to maximizing moonlight is close at hand.
I once read somewhere how to rearrange star dust.
I can experiment,
conjure beakers and Bunsen burners.
If that fails, I can dig up that citation.
Even if I can't pinpoint the whereabouts of kisses,
I honor your freckled hand caressing the mid-century book covers.
I amplify your tender whispers on the new anti-social media.
I polish the floors where your favorite armchair stood.
Never has your legacy been more resplendent.

צווישן די דאָזיקע ווערטער
דעמאַרקירט די זון די פֿאַרשיידנהייט
צווישן דעם רויט-ברוין פֿון דײַנע לאָקן
אונעם געל פֿון דײַן באָרד.
דו קוקסט אַרויף פֿון טרומייטן הילכנדיקע,
היפּטן וואָס שימיירן,
סאָפּראַנען וואָס טרילערן,
פֿאַרלייג אַ פֿוס איבער אַ פֿוס
און גיב מיר אַ שמייכל.

די ווילדע קאַץ וואָס האָסט געראַטעוועט פֿונעם הינטער געסל
קאָרטשעט זיך, אומרויִק אונטערן גלעט פֿון דײַן האַנט,
ניט אין שטאַנד אויסצוהאַלטן, ניט אין שטאַנד זיך אַוועק צו דרייען פֿון אַזאַ הנאה.
ווײַל געהאַט האָב איך קיין מאָל ניט אַזאַ מין אַמביוואַלענץ,
פֿאַרשטיי איך דעם נוצן, די נייטיקייט.
עפּעס ווייסט די קאַץ ניט צו קראַצן
די שפּינדלדיק-שטאַרקע קירשן האָלצערן פֿיס.
כ'האָב איר קיין מאָל קיין וואָרט ניט געזאָגט.
ס'איז קיין מאָל ניט געווען קיין צייט.
זי שאַרט זיך אַרײַן און אַרויס פֿון דײַן בײַזײַן—
פּונקט ווי זי טוט אינעם ליד אַליין.

דאָס ליד האָט מען געקענט זיך אויסמאָלן אין אַ שיין-באַפּוצטן צימער.
דער סוד פֿון מאַקסימיזירן לבֿנה-ליכט איז דערבײַ.
כ'האָב ערגעץ ווו אַ מאָל געלייענט ווי מע קען איבערשטעלן קאָסמישן שטויב.
כ'קען עקספּערימענטירן,
אַרויסרופֿן בעכערגלעזער און בונסען-ברענערס.
ווען ס'איז אומגעלונגען, קען איך אויסגראָבן דעם ציטאַט.
אַפֿילו ווען איך קען ניט טרעפֿן פּינקטלעך ווו קושן געפֿינען זיך,
גיב איך אָפּ כּבֿוד דײַן געשפּרענקלטער האַנט וואָס גלעט די ביכער טאָוולען פֿון מיטל-יאָרהונדערט.
איך פֿאַרשטאַרק דײַנע ליבלעכע שושקענישן אויף דער נײַער אַנטי-סאָציאַלער מעדיע.
איך פּוץ די פּאָדלאָגעס ווו ס'איז געשטאַנען דײַן באַליבסטער פֿאָטעל.
דײַן עזבֿון איז קיין מאָל מער פּראַקטיק ניט געווען.

פּיסאַ-מלוכה, מיט קאַץ

וואָלט איך געווען אין אַ קראָם פֿאַר געניצטע זאַכן,
וואָלט דער הינטערגרונט זיכער נאָר פֿאַרשטאַרקט דעם חן.
אַ יאָ, אָט איז די אוראַלטע נבֿיאהטע וואָס גיט מיר אַ שטורך פֿאָראויס.
דעם ספּעקטער פֿון האַנדלען וועט מען ניט אַרויסרופֿן.
די געשטעלן פֿון פּאַליעסטער העמדער און דינע שניפּסן און קליידלעך פֿון שיפֿאָן
און באַקעליט-געקנעפּלטע מאַנטלען פֿון יעגערהונט-ציין שטאָף,
און די איַינגערעמטע פּלאַקאַטן פֿון ראַק-און-ראָל שטערן אויף וואָס מע פֿלעגט
שטאַרבן,
וואָלט אַלץ זיך נאָכגעגעבן,
ביז די בליטשערס צוריקגעטראָטן.
די אַשן-פֿון-ראָז קנייטשן וואָלטן געגעבן אַ ווונק,
באַלויכטן מילד מײַן טאָג.

וואָלט איך געווען אין אַ מוזיי,
וואָלט עס געזעסן אויף אַ מיני-טריבונע.
אַ קרישטאָלע קאַראַפֿינקע וואָלט געקענט בלישטשען פּונקט צו רעכטס.
אינעם סאַמע לעצטן מאָמענט וואָלט איך צוריקגעצויגן די שפּיץ פֿינגער
פֿון די טיילעכלעך פֿון אָפּזעץ פֿון מעד וואָס איך האָב זיך דאָרט פֿאָרגעשטעלט.
עס וואָלט דאָ געווען אַ פּלאַקאַט וואָס וואָלט געלויבט זײַן פֿאָרעם—
סײַ זאַפֿטיק, סײַ מאָגער—
קלאָר צו מאַכן די פּאָזיציע אין דער געשיכטע פֿון בלענד.
אַנטקעגן דעם ווײַסקייט פֿון די ווענט
און דער געזעלשאַפֿט פֿון לאַנדסלײַט פֿון פֿריערדיקע תּקופֿות,
וואָלט עס זיכער אַרויסגערופֿן באַוווּנדער, ווי נאָר געמעסיקט.

ווען איך וואָלט געווען אין אַ היכלע,
וואָלטן פֿאַרבײַגייערס אפֿשר אויסגעגלאָצט אַן אויג ...,
צוגעצויגן פֿון פֿלאַמען וואָס צאַנקען אין ווײַנענדיקן גלאָז
און דער פֿאַרלײַטערונג פֿון אָנגענומענעם טרויער.
ווײַרעך-רויך וואָלט געקענט שוועבן אין דער לופֿטן.
בלומען פֿאַרשידנדיק פֿאַרוועלקט וואָלט מען געקענט אָנזען.
אין דער מראָקע
וועט מען ניט קענען וויסן אויף זיכער.
און אַפֿילו ווען מע וואָלט געקענט דעשיפֿרירן,
וואָלט מען ניט געטאָרט צוגיין,
כּאילו מיט אַ שטריך פֿון זיך אַליין צונויפֿגעדרייט איז עס אָפּקאָרדאָנירט.

אָבער מיר זײַנען דאָ אינעם ליד;
דאָס איז וואָס איז מיר געבליבן.

Fellow Travelers

The wind rustles through pines, birches, and others unnamed.
An owl's wings slash the smudges of charcoal.
Suddenly, night is sharpened into onyx.
Somewhere a mouse is surely seized and devoured.
Between wind and pursuit and downfall all you hear is silence.

You walk and walk,
although you can't remember donning these hiking boots.
You walk as if you were called here. And you were.
You've come a long way to this arboreal assembly.
You've sought out these hills, these strands of lushness.

This is where you've chosen to sculpt your conclusion.
Not in an institutional bed.
Not in bath tub water rapidly converting to crimson.
Not with pills strategically popped.
Not with a gun effortlessly acquired at the big box store.

Here in this renowned wood, where the air itself glows
as a kaleidoscope of green, darkness will rise.
You sense the spirits of those similarly inclined congregated around you.
You feel their wings drape over your shoulders.
Their cooing and whooshing adds to, rather than breaks, the silence.

Your shoulders slump into their collective presence.
Your body drops into the canopy of their arms.
Here finally you have found shelter.
The ghosts, your comrades, will usher you home.
On the peak of the North Star, the owl will ensure the bravura of your
crossing.

5 July 2017

מיטלויפֿערס

דער ווינט שאָרכעט דורך די סאָסנעס, בערעזעס, און אַנדערע
ניט-באַנאָמענטע.
די פֿליגלען פֿון אַ סאָווע שנײַדן דורך די שמירן פֿון האָלצקוילן.
פּלוצעם איז די נאַכט פֿאַרשאַרפֿט געוואָרן אין אָניקס אַרײַן.
ערגעץ ווו איז אַ מויז אַוודאי פֿאַרכאַפּט און אָפּגעפֿרעסט.
צווישן ווינט און נאָכיאָגן און אונטערגאַנג הערסטו נאָר שווײַגעניש.

דו גייסט און גייסט,
כאָטש דו קענסט ניט געדענקען ווען דו האָסט אָנגעטאָן די שפּאַציר-שטיוול.
דו גייסט אַזוי ווי מע האָט דיך אַהערפֿאַרבעטן. און מע האָט טאַקע.
דו ביסט אַ לאַנג וועג געקומען קיין אָט דעם בוים-אסיפֿה.
דו האָסט געזוכט אָט די בערגלעך, די שנירלעך רײַכקייט.

דעם אָרט האָסט אויסגעקליבן צו סקולפּטירן דײַן סוף.
ניט אין קיין אינסטיטוציאָנעלן-בעט.
ניט אין קיין וואַנע-וואַסער וואָס ווערט אין גיכן רויט.
ניט מיט פּילן ברייטהאַרציק אײַנגעשלונגען.
ניט מיט קיין פּיסטויל גריגערהייט געקויפֿט אין אַ "גרויס-קעסטל-געשעפֿט."

דאָ אינעם באַרימטן וואַלד ווו די לופֿט אַליין גליט
ווי אַ קאַלײַדאָסקאָפּ פֿון גרין ווען דאָס פּינצטערניש אויפֿשטיין.
אַרום דיר דערפֿילסטו דעם פֿאַרזאַמלן זיך פֿון ענלעכע רוחות.
דו פֿילסט זייערע פֿליגלען דראַפּירן אויף דײַנע אַקסלען.
זייערע טאָרקלען און זיפֿצן געבן צו, אַנשטאָט צעברעכן, דאָס שווײַגעניש.

דײַנע אַקסלען שטייען אײַנגעבויגן אין זייער קאָלעקטיוון בײַזײַן.
דײַן גוף פֿאַלט אַרײַן אינעם באַלדאַכין פֿון זייערע אָרעמס.
דאָ האָסטו סוף-כּל-סוף געפֿונען אַ מקום-מיקלט.
די רוחות, דיינע חבֿרים, וועלן דיך אַהיימבאַגלייטן.
אויפֿן שפּיץ פֿונעם פֿאָלאַר-שטערן וועט דער סאָווע גאַראַנטירן
די פּראַכט פֿון אײַער איבערגאַנג.

דעם 5טן יולי 2017

II. Black Blots Blast into Blue Baklava

Litany/ies: October, Long Past Millennium's Turn

He said: You need to do more.
What you are doing is well and good,
but I can't see this long term.
You know—a future.
Moving in together,
or any kind of durable partnering, for that matter.

Never mind the difference in décor.
Your fixation on a dot in the middle of the last century.
Albeit, an influential dot.
Well, we're in a new century—millennium—I mean.
Y2k turned out okay.
The long clean lines have evolved. You need to, too.

The lines are just a bit bulkier now.
You need to be, too.
There's room for pops of ornamentation.
Make room.
There's space here.
Never mind all that "clean."

You need to cook. You need to control the calories.
That polyglot palate of yours: Thai today, Burmese tomorrow,
Mexican the next, Middle Eastern after that.
I'm not a food nationalist. But what are you?
A single-stomach culinary UN?
Fine. So be it, but be it here. In the garret.

You need to anchor your palate.
Touch and manipulate the ingredients
you like to fondle at the farmers' market.
Be kosher, not as the rabbis want, but as in kashrut of the self.
Know what's entering your body. Always a good strategy,
and not just with food. Guard the temple.

Contact the urban gardeners.
You can't exist on take-out forever.
You won't always be in the metropolis,
where so many come to escape,

to thrive.
Sanctuary city, yes.

There will be a time when there is no metropolis.
It will have been nearly emptied. Reconfigured. Or deserted.
I see a day.
What will you do in the forest?
There is sustenance to be foraged.
There are secrets on and in the forest floor. Forage!

So what if the yeshiva didn't have boy scouts?
There are scouts for adults.
Don't we (also) revere the Baal Shem Tov for his reveries in the forest?
Do you think he was just communing/cleaving with the Divine?
Trust me: He had his eye on the ground, too.
So no excuses.

I cannot live like this.
You can't either.
But you know what?
It's more than that.
It's less.
You need to put out more.

I don't care how good your mouth is.
Oral isn't enough.
I came of age at the same time you did.
Get over it.
There are meds now.
It's past the aughts.

And you ought to know better.
So there was a foundational crucible.
A big deal, yes. But it can be shed or even just rattled.
Make a new crucible.
The plague may not be over, but it's at bay.
Or, at least, it could be.

Be grateful for what's available to you.
So there were other things that happened. That was a long time ago.
There are alternatives to the albatross paradigm of history.
Why not bloom in the here?
This offering … this moment … won't last long.
Hell, I sure won't.

I'm outta here. Adios! Hang onto that toothbrush.
It's a new season. Autumn.
I'll see you in the bars or the baths or the brambles
or wherever it is that I'll see you.
Don't look away.
Remember this that I'm telling you.

Remember that night you came to my place.
Remember the red light of my dark room. My innermost sanctum.
Our red kiss. Our red embrace. Remember that Communards song
from *Red* that I played for you the night we met.
It turns out I could say goodbye. How I caressed that red album cover
when I removed the record. How I caressed you, the feathery of you.

Remember vinyl?
Remember what you could have had if you'd stayed with me.
If you had given more. If you had let us be more. More… More red.
Remember me. Remember us.
Dear one, remember the commune's light.
Forget not our Communard night.

(Fraternal) Twin Meditations on the Theme of Tenacity

1.

Minimalism had always been a goal. Classical proportions of a fine flat not far from the city center. A sofa, a few chairs, a bed, a writing desk, a table, a closet or two. What else was needed for a life of the mind, whether solitary or not? Beyond the basics, what need of things? And that minimalism stayed vivid, burned fervent. Only life had a way of meddling, as they say, and advertising, for all his aloofness and derision, had sticky tentacles. Consumerist neon flashed bright over the fingers hovering above the remote-control buttons and keyboards. Clothes, lotions, art pottery. But mostly the books. As the years evolved, it became harder to discard books. Like the sacred books gifted to him for his bar mitzvah, which he never opened, much less read. Still, the idea of them appealed. The scholar contributing commentaries on the canon, entering links into the golden chain. And the secular ones. And too, the ones that refused such a dichotomy. The ones for the undergraduate Radicalism in America class. The American social novel. The monographs from the senior historiography seminar. The texts from the undergraduate women's history class taken for graduate credit. The first intellectual and political forays out of the claustrophobic restrictions of stricture and piety and the what seem liked thousands of thou-shalt-not's. The remembered conversations outside of class when we looked at the past to find a way into a future both grand and possible. Conversations hopeful but always tempered by reality. For all his efforts at detachment, these texts lining his garret could not help but remind him of that time of excitement, of hope, of shaping a new generation of students. And then there were the inscribed books exchanged with other writers. Surely, those had to stay! Still, some were released, liberated from his clutches. He did make an effort at downsizing or decluttering, dutifully taking them to the few book sales or organizations that would have them. But most stayed in the garret, along the white-painted shelf already present when he first moved in, one of the selling features of the garret in the first place. And their number never really seemed to diminish. The bulk of the books stayed, testament to the durability of a dream, textual talismans of lifelong intellectual undertaking. To live with ideas and art. For enrichment of the soul. Not in the world to come, but for the here, for the life lived in this garret. This cloister. Not far from the monastery. The education of an invert. The education of an introvert. The education of an introverted invert.

2.

Years, multiple decades after this education, and in fact, mere hours before writing this meditation, he heard an interview of a daring if curmudgeonly writer/director who went to great lengths to film in remote and dangerous locations, who scorned award shows and resisted the probing for personal introspection presented by the interviewer. Even as his oeuvre delved into the dark recesses of the human soul, he himself resisted turning that scalpel on himself. Still, there was plenty of material for the listener to work with, to forge into imagining. Even if he wouldn't, the listener could, if not do it for him, at least imagine it. At least the outlines. As he folded his laundry—underwear here, casuals there—he considered his own project. Writing the unwritable, or rather, the writable with determination. He wondered about the "healing" aspects of such writing. The rummaging around in the darkness. The piles. The central moments. The black light bulbs of hell. The purgatory beyond. Was there a light in the middle, let alone, at the end? The fear, not exactly of being cancelled, but of being marginalized, pigeonholed. Pitied. Yes, there was a light. Surely, there was, despite the declarations of the aforementioned writer/director. There had to be, he insisted to himself. The body in pain so agonizing he could barely walk, had to crawl to the loo. Even though there was nothing "wrong" with his body. Or nothing that the many doctors could uncover, in any case. The body didn't want him to remember—anything but that! Don't go there! Shut it down. Turn away, pirouette like the director in the interview. The body tried to distract him—look at this bright shiny agony here instead! He might have continued to do so were it not for the healers who guided him back into the heart of darkness. It is possible to look and to return. And so he did. And so he has. Still, the body holds the secrets. The body never forgets. The body knows not of time. Yesterday is today. The mind races, works to accrete, but the body just knows. Someday, some night, stars and moon embracing overhead, mind and body will meet. And rest together.

Bebop Blues/Lullaby Ghost

It happened to him at all of the predictable times.
This grip of longing,
the ache of absence.
When he went to family gatherings,
where he was the only member not tending little ones.
Now his great-nieces & nephews are having little ones of their own.
Tick-tock; tock-tick.

When he was sitting on a park bench,
and the young mothers came by.
Giving him space.
Cosmos in which to breathe.
Aging cosmonaut queen flying, or fluttering, solo.
No ladies in waiting here.
Don't want what he has. Or hasn't, as it were.

Or the nannies. Wheeling the babes barely visible
save the signifier of blue or pink (or sometimes yellow) flashing by,
but still weighty, given the Cadillac carriages gleaming in the
afternoon sun.
Or the older ones dressed to the nines, in the little strollers.
Sailor suit. Cap. Little dandy!
Lace dress. Ribbons. Tiny diva!
Even if the finery didn't stay fine for long. Stain and slobber have a
way.

Then the tantrums.
Throwing the toy,
slamming it to the ground,
wanting a different one,
a better one, the only one now out of reach.
The one left at the home.
The toy that will make all right in the world.

The nannies conferring,
over this or that boss
and the child they'd once tended
who'd been such an angel,
unlike this one here.

Sour puss!
Once, a nanny weeping silently into her handkerchief.

He'd been a nanny, too.
Well, a babysitter, really.
Backing up his sister as needed.
So he knows a thing a too about tending the child not one's own.
Still, this is different.
This nanny cannot be without that reference.
What assumptions he makes about the lives of others!

What an eavesdropper he is.
Oznayim la-kotel. The walls have ears. Except he's no wall.
Just flesh and blood who has not fulfilled his duty.
As it is stated in the Bible Genesis 1:28: *Peru u-revu.* Be fruitful and multiply.
Are you any different?
Are you better than Adam and Eve?
Be fruitful, you fruit. Thou who art fruit.

Tutty-fruity, oh rootie,
insisted Little Richard.
Who adopted a child,
not so by the way.
You could, too.
There's still time.
Tick-tock. Tock-tick.

So what if you don't have a gal named
Sue or Daisy?
Or, for that matter,
Blume or Rinah?
Maybe adoption would count,
even if you're not furthering the blood line.
The rabbis could tell you. If you'd only ask.

And why didn't you?
Never mind.
You still can.

So many children waiting, hoping.
More than the blood line, the traditions.
The ways of our people.
The people.

The nation needs you.
We are under siege.
There is an Amalek in every generation.
When has there not been one?
Do not forsake the edicts of the texts, for sure.
But mostly, the needs of the nation.
Do not embrace the apostasy of this chosen barrenness.

But he thinks about the aforementioned grip of longing,
that barrenness in unexpected places, too.
The grocery store.
The buying for one.
The conference presentation.
The conference organizing.
The inclusion of story hour for the little ones.

The demagogues droning on about family values.
Did he not have family, too?
Blood or chosen.
However configured, still family.
Network of love. Net of love.
Catch me if—when—I fall. Propel me to rise.
The Friday nights. The Saturday nights. The high holidays.

The holidays.
The sukkah hopping that will never be.
The seder. O the youngest for the recitation of the *Mah nishtanah!*
The movement of days, the structure of calendar.
Tick-tock. Tock-tick.
The ritual—always familiar,
never the same.

When is there not this longing?
When is there not this absence?

When is there not a crib envisioned?
When does he not wish he could sing
        Shlof, mayn kind/Sleep, my child?
Wop bop a loo bop a lop bom bom the lullaby, sweet baby.
It's a mash-up. Homage to Little Richard, little one.

In the cabaret, with its spare instrumentation,
the lullaby is realized.
From smoke and wine, he heads home.
Walks the stone bridge swaying in the fortress of frost.
Specters of small arms tangle themselves around him at the door.
Next to bachelor bed, the baby monitor detects a stirring,
blinks red from the next room.

Milk and Honey Moon Harvest

Nights are hard, Mother.
The dark is relentless, offers no reprieve.
The moon reveals only the moons beneath my eyes.
The north star is lost among the confetti in the heavens.
Where is its twinkle?
Where is its famed brightness that will lead us into the Promised Land?

The promised land you never saw is at my bedside. Our bedsides.
Even as the holy wall graced the cover of your green prayerbook.
Even as the blue and white box for national renewal filled with coins.
Peace.
The word buzzes purple on the shelves of the props room behind the
        world stage.
There can be tranquility, insist the visionaries with clenched teeth.

Arguments, quarrels, wringings of hand aren't inevitable, either.
There were moments free from those.
Whole days of respite. Devoid of despair.
When we were all together around the Sabbath table.
When the aroma of *tsholnt* spread throughout the house
and its potatoes carrots barley beef dispersed magic through our bellies.

And in that way, the Day of Rest lived up to its name.
The miracle of rest that so eludes me now.
And you all those years.
Oh, Mother,
you never got to taste
the milk and honey flowing from the source.

Barley, figs, dates, pomegranates, etc.
All of the seven kinds.
The seven wonders.
Bounty of the land

Directly from God's hands.
Did God run out?

Did His hands tremble when it came to you?
Every inch of the land contested.
Someday there will be peace. It is not a pie in the sky.
Nor is it one of your Lady Baltimore cakes on the butler's pantry sideboard.
There are those who are searching for an answer.
Just as you did. Someday I will find peace, Mother.

Nights are hard, Mother.
The catastrophic state of things.
Invasions. Rapes. Massacres. Beheadings. Bombings. Rockets. Displacements.
The hostages. The refugees. The tent cities. The dead. The…
It wasn't always like this. It won't always be, right?
The cards don't tell us. The palm reader lowers her eyes in avoidance.

You should have gotten to kiss the sand.
It would have reciprocated, sure of your tenderness.
Your tears would have dried between its particles.
Your heart would have slowed in the embrace of Rachel's Tomb,
Your needlework of those walls adorns this garret.
Memento of our matriarch Rachel. Memento of Mother.

You should still be here. With us. Be with us still, Mother.
Shhh. You are.
The Lady Baltimore cake has cooled down.
Beneath the eight gables,
the moons beneath my eyes expand, vibrate.
Do you sense the vibrations, Mother?

The coins in the blue and white metal box are rattling.
How can I possibly sleep with their racket?
Instead of milk and honey, this milky brew of incongruous conflation.
Instead of barley, figs, dates, pomegranates, etc.,
only these words in search of the north star.
Mother, help me locate, help me reveal, the brightness.

דירעקט פֿונעם אייבערשטנס הענט.
צי זײַנען זיי בײַם אייבערשטן אויסגעגאַנגען?

צי האָבן זײַנע הענט געציטערט לגבי דיר?
יעדער אמה פֿון דער ערד אָפּגעפֿרעגט.
אַ מאָל וועט זײַן שלום. ס'איז ניט קיין טעלערל פֿון הימל.
צי דײַנס אַ "לײדי באָלטימאָר"-קוכן וועלכער שטייט
    אויף דעם הויז-באַדינערס-שפּײַזאַרניע-בופֿעט.
פֿאַראַן אַזוינע וואָס זוכן אַן ענטפֿער.
פונקט אַזוי ווי דו האָסט געזוכט. אַ מאָל וועל איך געפֿינען שלום, מאַמע.

די נעכט זײַנען האַרב, מאַמע.
דער קאַטאַסטראָפֿישער מצבֿ פֿון דער וועלט.
די אינוואַזיעס. די פֿאַרגוואַלדיקנגען. די הריגות. די קעפּנונגען. די ראַקעטן.
    די באָמבאַדירונגען. די פֿאַרשטויסן.
די געפֿאַנגענע. די פּליטים. די געצעלטשטעט. די טויטע. די...
ס'איז נישט אַלע מאָל געווען אַזוי. ס'וועט נישט אַלע מאָל זײַן אַזוי, אַיאָ?
די קאָרטן זאָגן גאָרנישט. די כיראָמאַנטקע לאָזט אַראָפּ די אויגן
    אין בכּווינדיקער אויסמײַדונג.

דו האָסט געזאָלט קענען קושן דאָס זאַמד.
דאָס זאַמד וואָלט דיר געהאַט צוריקגעקושט, זיכער מיט דײַן צרטלעכקייט.
דײַנע טרערן וואָלטן געהאַט אויסגעטריקנט געוואָרן צווישן זײַנע שטײַבעלעך.
דײַן האַרץ וואָלט זיך געהאַט פֿאַרפֿאַמעלכט אינעם אַרומנעם פֿון קבֿר-רחל.
דײַן נאָדל-אַרבעט פֿון יענע ווענט באַפּוצט מײַן בוידעמשטיבל.
אָנדענק פֿון רחל אמנו. אָנדענק פֿון דער מאַמען.

דו האָסט געזאָלט דאָ נאָך אַלץ זײַן. מיט אונדז. זײַ נאָך אַלץ מיט אונדז, מאַמע.
שש־שאַ. דו ביסט יאָ דאָ.
דער "לײדי באָלטימאָר"-קוכן האָט זיך שוין אָפּגעקילט.
אונטער די אַכט דאַכשפּיצן,
פֿאַרברייטערן זיך, וויברירן די לבֿנות אונטער מײַנע אויגן.
צי דערשפּירסטו די וויבראַציעס, מאַמע?

די מטבעות אינעם בלויע־און־ווייסן מעטאַלענעם קעסטל קלאַפּערן.
סטײַטש—ווי אַזוי קען איך שלאָפֿן אין מיטן אַזאַ רעש?
אַנשטאָט מילך און האָניק, אָט די אויסבריִונג פֿונעם
    נישט-צוגעפּאַסטן צונויפֿקאָס.
אַנשטאָט גערשט, פֿײַגן, טײַטלען, מילגרוימען, אאַ"ו,
נאָר די ווערטער אויפֿן וועג צו געפֿינען דעם צפֿון-שטערן.
מאַמע, העלף מיר געפֿינען, העלף מיר אַנטפּלעקן, די העלקייט.

מילך־און־האָניקדיקע לבֿנה־האַרבסטונג

די נעכט זיינען האַרב, מאַמע.
דאָס פֿינצטערניש איז אומדערבאַרעמדיק, דערלאַנגט
ניִשט קיין לינדערונג.
די לבֿנה אַנטפּלעקט נאָר די לבֿנות אונטער מײַנע אויגן.
דעם צפֿון-שטערן קען מען נישט געפֿינען צווישן די קאָנפֿעטי
אין די הימלען.
ווּ איז זײַן פֿינקל?
ווּ איז זײַן באַרימטער העלקייט וואָס וועט אונדז פֿירן אינעם
צוגעזאָגטן לאַנד אַרײַן?

דאָס צוגעזאָגטער לאַנד וואָס דו האָסט קיין מאָל נישט געזען שטייט בײַ מײַן בעט.
בײַ אונדזערע בעטן.
אַפֿילו ווען די הייליקע וואַנט האָט באַשײַנט דעם טאָוול פֿון דײַן גרינעם סידור.
אַפֿילו ווען דאָס בלוי־און־ווײַסע קעסטל אויף נאַציאָנאַלער באַנײַונג
איז געווען פֿול מיט מטבעות.
שלום.
דאָס וואָרט זשומעט פערפל אויף די פּאָליצעס פֿונעם רעקוויזיט-צימער
הינטער דער וועלטבינע.
שלווה איז מעגלעך, שפּאַרן זיך אײַן די וויזיאָנערן מיט די צונויפֿגעדריקטע ציין.

מחלוקתן, קריגערייען, און הענט־פּאַרברעכונג זײַנען אויך נישט אומפֿאַרמײַדלעך.
עס זיינען געווען מאָמענטן אָן זיי.
גאַנצע טעג פֿון אָטעם-אָנכאַפּ. אָן פֿאַרצווייפֿלונג.
ווען מיר זײַנען אַלע געזעסן אַרום דעם שבת טיש.
ווען דער ריח פֿון טשאָלנט האָט זיך פֿאַרשפּרייט דורכן הויז
און זײַנע קאַרטאָפֿל, מערן, גערשט, פֿלייש האָבן פֿאַרשפּרייט
כּישוף דורך אונדזערע בײַכער.

און אַזוי טאַקע האָט דער יום מנוחה אונדז נישט אַנטוישט.
דער נס פֿון מנוחה וואָס גליטשט זיך אַרויס איצט פֿון מיר.
און פֿון דיר אויך דורך די אַלע יאָרן.
אוי, מאַמע,
דו האָסט קיין מאָל נישט זוכה געווען צו פֿאַרזוכן
די מילך און דעם האָניק וואָס פֿליסן פֿונעם קוואַל.

גערשטן, פֿײַגן, טײַטלען, מילגרוימען, אאַ״וו.
די אַלע שיבֿעה־מינים.
די שיבֿעה וווּנדערס.
די שפֿע פֿונעם לאַנד

Midrash on a Gravestone Acrostic Inscription

((long) after an August 29, 2012 visit to Beth Israel Cemetery, Woodbridge, New Jersey)

There were no weeds. No flowers, either. Never flowers. Only pebbles as precarious as crown. The rocks below were combed. The grass was luxuriant. (For a moment, I wanted to roll in it.) Rolling. In another context, meadows. Might still be, for all I know. I haven't been back. But still, I was there. So long ago. Am there. Only the sun was punishing. Garish in glare. I fumbled with prayers. Blessings? Sister knew what to recite. Where to go. How to be. This wasn't her first rodeo. And there you are separated from your father who passed young, too. Even in eternal rest, the genders may not mingle.

אשה יראת ה' צנועה וחסודה
Ishah yir'at H. tsenu'ah va-hasudah
A woman God-fearing, modest, and kind
Yes. Yes. And yes. Who could disagree? Not I.

רציוה ונאמנה לרבים היתה
***R**etsuyah ve-ne'emanah le-rabim haytah*
Sought-after by and loyal to the public
Myself included. When always you believed in me. In us. That I could finish this assignment on time. That I could participate in the science fair. I didn't want to stay away from this place.

ידיה פעלו להחזקת התורה
***Y**adeha po'olo le-hahzakat ha-Torah*
Her hands worked to strengthen the Torah
That it was okay to not excel at baseball. When did your hands rest from God's work?
Even in rest, they moved. Twitching, then reaching, for the next task.

יסוד בתינו ישבה באהלה
***Y**esod batenu yashvah be-oholah*
The foundation of our house was in her tent
Yes, you sat humbly in the tent. Plainly. Like Jacob, ish tam, a "man of simplicity/innocence/wholeness," who sat in the tent. Ishah temimah. The tent has walls. The tent's flap is easy to open. Strangers are welcome. For, even if you sometimes may have wished you had a bit more prior notice, when didn't you welcome the yeshiva student to your home-cooked meal?

And yes, we have a spare room. A room that was spare. And yes, plain, also. Small but comfortable. The golden curtains salute the sun. Mornings will find you eager. No matter the dust from the long and winding freeway, no traveler left your tent weary.

זיכתה אחרים להיות לעזרה
Zikhtah aherim li-heyot le-ʿazarah
She encouraged caused motivated others to be a help
To be for help. She fostered an atmosphere of help. Righteousness rightness shall ye pursue. To know the power within to be of help. Do good in the world. No scale too small.

לעולם לא נשכח נשמתה הטהורה
Le-ʿolam lo nishkah nishmatah ha-tehorah
Her pure soul will never be forgotten
No, it won't. Not before this monument or elsewhere. Wherever we go, she goes.
Whither thou goest … Yes, Book of Ruth. Book of Ruth/Reyzl.

מסרה נפשה לגדל בניה לתורה
Masrah nafshah le-gadel baneha le-Torah
She gave her life to raise her children for Torah
Yes, and even if we didn't and still don't live up to her sacrifice, she still gave it. Even with all that was denied her, all that she yearned for but never received, she never stopped urging, ushering her children to Torah.

I came to battle these words. Those new ancient words. What could they offer? How could they capture the delicacy of her devotion? The loss that never that never blunted the love. The magnetism, the loyalty and friendships she inspired. How, even after the battles, even after the rage, she never lost faith. The anchor.

Instead, I enter them. These enstoned words. Inhabit them. Take them with me. The wind gales barrel them close. I retain my footing. This glare won't always be. The ghosts can slip between the monuments at midnight. Dance even. When the moon is nearly full. Or when it's not. Picnics before dawn are a possibility. A necessity. Inquire at the front office for options.

Engraved on stone. Engraved in memory. Engraved in community. Engraved-on-grave. The rabbis' wives' recount her legend. The rabbis, too. The rabbis could have dictated the lines into engravement. A consortium assembled in the clouds. A lone rabbi? Perhaps the angels did. Perhaps God above saw to them … or took up the engraving quill Himself. Or perhaps the whippoorwills offered them to the wind when the dark and the quiet weren't enough? Perhaps the wind? Engraved into wind. Engraved onto the lost women's auxiliary cookbook pages. In *tsholnts* past and present and of all time. So much engraving, so many places of engravement, and still the squish-squash of this swamp. Still, this sorrow.

אײַנגעקריצט אויף שטיין. אײַנגעקריצט אין זכּרון. אײַנגעקריצט אין קהילה. אײַנגעגראָבן אין גרוב אַרײַן. די רביצינס דערציילן איר לעגענדע. די רביים דערציילן אויך. די רביים האָבן געקענט דיקטירן די שורות אין אײַנגעגריצקייט. אַ קאָנסאָרציום פֿאַרזאַמלט אין די וואָלקנס. איין רבי אַליין? אפֿשר האָבן די מלאכים דאָס געטאָן. אפֿשר האָט גאָט געמאַכט אַז זיי זאָלן... אָדער אפֿשר האָט גאָט אַליין אויפֿגעהויבן די אײַנקריצונג- געגנדזענע פען. אָדער אפֿשר האָבן די שרײַענדיקער ציגן-מעלקערס זיי דערלאַנגט דעם ווינט ווען דאָס פֿינצטערניש און די שטילקייט זײַנען נישט געווען גענוג. אפֿשר דער ווינט אַליין? אײַנגעקריצט אין ווינט אַרײַן. אײַנגעקריצט אויף די זײַטן פֿונעם פֿאַרלוירענעם קאָכבוך פֿון דעם פֿרויען-קאָמיטעט ״נשי אַגודת ישׂראל״. אין טשאָלנטן פֿאַרגאַנגענע און איצטיקע און פֿון אַלע צײַטן. אַזוי פֿיל אײַנקריצן, אַזוי פֿיל ערטער פֿון אײַנקריצונג, און דאָך דאָס צעקוועטש-פּליוך פֿונעם זומפּ דאָ. דאָך, דער טרויער.

און יאָ, האָבן מיר אַן איבעריקן צימער. אַ צימער וואָס איז געווען צימצומדיק. און יאָ, פּראָסט און פּשוט אויך. קליין, אָבער באַקוועם. די גאָלדענע פֿאָרהאַנגען סאַלוטירן די זון. אין דער פֿרי טרעפֿט מען דיך זשעדנע. נישט געקוקט אויפֿן שטויב פֿונעם לאַנגן, שלענגלדיקן שאָסיי איז קיין פֿאַרבײַפֿאָרער נישט אַוועק פֿון דײַן געצעלט אַ נישט־אָפּגערוטער.

זיכתה אחרים להיות לעזרה
זי האָט דערמוטיקט, מאָטיווירט אַנדערע צו זײַן אַ הילף
צו זײַן צו הילף. זי האָט קולטיווירט אַ הילפֿס-סבֿיבֿה. *צדק צדק תרדוף*. צו קענען דעם
כּח וואָס געפֿינט זיך אינעווייניק צו זײַן אַ הילף. גוט זאָלט איר טאָן אין דער וועלט.
קיין וואָג נישט צו קליין.

לעולם לא נשכח נשמתה הטהורה
איר ריינע נשמה וועט קיין מאָל נישט פֿאַרגעסן ווערן
ניין, ס'וועט נישט. נישט פֿאַר אָט דער מצבֿה און נישט ערגעץ אַנדערש. וווּהין מיר גייען, גייט זי אונדז מיט. וווּהין דו
גייסט... יאָ, מגילת רות. מגילת רות/רייזל.

מסרה נפשה לגדל בניה לתורה
זי האָט געווידמעט איר לעבן דעם אויסכאָווען אירע קינדער אין דער תּורה
יאָ, און אַפֿילו ווען מיר האָבן נישט אויסגעהאַלטן און עד היום האַלטן נישט אויס איר מסירת-נפֿש, דאָך האָט זי אים
פֿרײַ געגעבן. אַפֿילו מיט אַלץ וואָס מע האָט איר נישט צוגעלאָזט, אַלץ וואָס זי האָט געוואָלט אָבער קיין מאָל נישט
באַקומען, האָט זי קיין מאָל נישט אויפֿגעהערט אונטערטרײַבן, באַגלייטן די קינדער צו דער תּורה.

געקומען בין איך צו באַקעמפֿן אָט די ווערטער. יענע נײַע אַנטיקע ווערטער. וואָס האָבן זיי געקענט דערלאַנגען? ווי אַזוי האָבן זיי געקענט כאַפּן די איידלקייט פֿון איר איבערגעבנקייט? דעם אָנווער וואָס האָט נישט געקענט אָפּטעמפּן די ליבשאַפֿט. די צוציִקראַפֿט, די געטרײַשאַפֿט, און די פֿרײַנדשאַפֿט וואָס זי האָט איספּירירט. ווי, אַפֿילו נאָך די אַלע שלאַכטן, אַפֿילו נאָכן כּעס, האָט זי קיין מאָל נישט פֿאַרלוירן אמונה. דעם אַנקער.

אַנשטאָט קאַמף גיי איך אין די ווערטער אַרײַן. אָט די פֿאַרשטיינערטע ווערטער. כ'ווױן אין זיי. כ'נעם זיי מיט. די שטורעמווינטן האַקן זיי נאָענט. כ'האַלט דעם באָדן אונטער די פֿיס. דער בליִאַסק וועט נישט אַלע מאָל זײַן. די רוחות קענען פֿאַרפֿליען צווישן די מצבֿות בײַ חצות. טאַנצן אַפֿילו. ווען די לבֿנה איז אַ פֿולע. און ווען זי איז נישט. פּיקניקן פֿאַר עלות-השחר זײַנען אויך מעגלעך. אַ מוז־זאַך. פֿרעג בײַם אַדמיניסטריר-ביוראָ נאָך ברירות.

מדרש וועגן אַ מצבֿה-אַקראָסטיך-אײַנשריפֿט

((לאַנג) נאָך אַ וויזיט פֿונעם 29סטן אויגוסט 2012 אינעם בית-ישׂראל בית-עולם, וודברידזש, ניו-דזשערזי)

קיין ווילדגראָז איז נישט געווען. קיין בלומען אויך נישט. קיין מאָל נישט בלומען. נאָר שטיינדלעך וואַקלדיק ווי אַ קרוין. די שטיינער אונטן האָט מען צוגעקעמט. דאָס גראָז איז געווען געדיכט. (אויף אַ רגע האָב איך געוואָלט זיך קײַקלען אויף דעם.) קײַקלען זיך. אין אַן אַנדערן קאָנטעקסט, לאָנקעס. דאָס געדיכטע גראָז קען נאָך אַלץ זײַן, לויט אויף וויפֿל איך ווייס. כ'בין קיין מאָל נישט צוריק. אָבער דאָך בין איך דאָרטן געווען. מיט אַזוי פֿיל יאָרן צוריק. בין נאָך אַלץ דאָרט. אָבער די זון איז געווען האַרב. רײַסיק מיט איר בליאַסק. ~~כ'האָב זיך געפֿאָרקעט מיט די תפֿילות:~~ ברכות? די שוועסטער האָט געוווּסט וואָס מע דאַרף רעציטירן. וווּהין צו גיין. וויאַזוי צו פֿירן זיך. ס'איז נישט געווען איר ערשטער וויזיט. און דאָרטן ביסטו אָפּגעזונדערט פֿון דײַן טאַטן וואָס איז אויך יונג אַוועק פֿון דער וועלט. אַפֿילו אין אייביקן רו טאָרן די מינים נישט אויסמישן זיך.

אשה יראת ה' צנועה וחסודה
אַ פֿרוי וואָס האָט מורא פֿון גאָט, באַשיידנדיק, און האַרציק
יאָ. יאָ. און יאָ. ווער וועט נישט מסכּים זײַן? נישט איך.

רצויה ונאמנה לרבים היתה
געוווּנטשן און געטרײַ פֿאַרן עולם
מיך אַרײַנבעמענדיק. אין מיר האָסטו אַלע מאָל געגלויבט. אין אונדז. אַז איך וועל קענען ענדיקן דעם היימאַרבעט צו דער צײַט. אַז איך וועל קענען אָנטיילנעמען אינעם וויסנשאַפֿט-יאַריד. איך האָב נישט געוואָלט אַוועקשטיין פֿונעם אָרט.

ידיה פעלו להחזקת התורה
אירע הענט האָבן געאַרבעט אויף צו פֿאַרשטאַרקן די תּורה
נישט אויסצייכענען זיך מיט בייסבאָל איז אויך געווען גוט. ווען האָבן דײַנע הענט גענומען אַ הפֿסקה פֿון גאָטס אַרבעט? אַפֿילו אין רו, האָבן זיי זיך באַוועגט. מיטצוקן, זיך אויסשטרעקן צו דער קומעדיקער עבֿודה.

יסוד בתינו ישבה באָהלה
דער פֿונדאַמענט פֿון אונדזער הויז איז געווען אין איר געצעלט
יאָ, עניוות׳דיק ביסטו זיך געזעסן אינעם געצעלט. סתם אַזוי. אַזוי ווי יעקבֿ, איש תּם, אַ "מאַן פֿון פּשטות/ריײניקייט/תּמימות," איז געזעסן אינעם געצעלט. אשה תּמימה. דאָס געצעלט האָט וועגט. דאָס עפֿענען דעם געצעלטס צודעקל איז גרינג. פֿרעמדע זײַנען אײַנגעלאַדן. ס'טײַטש, אַפֿילו ווען דו האָסט אַ מאָל געוואָלט וויסן אַ ביסל מער אין פֿאָראויס וועגן די וויזיטן, ווען האָסט נישט שיין אויפֿגענומען אַ ישיבֿה בחור אויף אַ היימיש-געקאָכטער מאָלצײַט?

Peace/Pieces of Mind

I.

Come to take the waters. Partake of them. Our town is not renowned for them, but they are there. And they are not far from where you can be staying. Will be staying? Impossible to know now for how long. Yes, there will be guided excursions to the waters. See: our windows open onto the mountains. No, they are not barred. Well, some of them are. But only those that need to be. Look at how easily these ones here open. That's right, just a flick of the handle. Step out onto the limestone balconies. There are many to choose from. Isn't the carving exquisite? No, you certainly can't find that kind of artistry anymore. The skill sets aren't there. Nor the commitment. As you can see, we have worked to preserve the grandeur. But our standards within have been updated since the founding. The attendants will guide you onto the balconies if you're feeling unsure. If you need a nudge or a bit of coaxing. Yes, we call them attendants. We prefer that over other titles. That is what they do—attend to your needs. We look for a certain circumspection in our attendants. A strength of character. And of body … in case that's needed. In case things get "out of hand." Which we hope they won't … and don't expect them to. Glorious, isn't it all? Quietly so. Our "physical plant," I mean. For the purposes at hand, that is. Hopefully, not "over the top." You know, we don't usually resort to speaking in quotes so much, but sometimes it's just what's needed. "Resort"—not an accidental word choice, eh? This is a kind of resort, isn't it? Sometimes, these expressions are just useful. The words of the people. But yes, discretion is really what we've aimed for. And notions of discretion have shifted over time. That can't be helped. But you can trust us.

II.

Never you mind the cannon fire in the distance. It'll simmer down. Or it won't. Either way, it won't affect us. The general will stay away from us. What's he called—the Commander?—has seen to that. And if he doesn't, well, we're figure something out. We don't have an inflated sense of our influence, but we've always been resourceful. We think you'll enjoy your stay. However long it may be. However long it needs to be. You'll know when it's time to come. And when it's time to leave. You'll get help with both of those decisions. We'll see to that. Our experts will. Don't be fooled by their white coats. They're all very approachable. Relaxed even. The way you would be if you were here. Pioneering, they are, open to all the latest methodologies, but also steeped in tradition. And our rooms are comfortable. Let's have a look. We might as well. We're here, aren't we? They're equipped to be unequipped. Safety in simplicity. Minimalism = restoration. These are just a few of our mottoes. Our food, too, is plain. But nurturing. Tasty but without agitation-inducing spices. This is not a place where agitation is encouraged or in any way nurtured. In nature will you be at one with, and indeed, nurtured by, nature, we like to say.

III.

Come to take the waters. Partake of them. As I've said, our town is not renowned for them, but they are here. That's right, step away from the balcony edge now. And down this path we go. Feel the closeness of the pines. You do have to keep your sandals on here, but you can still enjoy the pine needle carpet. They're there for you. Feel the water's freshness, the cool of its clean. Immerse yourself. Cleanse all that came before. It will still be there. Only cleaner. Yes, here's a towel now. Easy does it. You've got this. We're so glad you decided to come. Or it was decided. Yes, the decision has been documented. We still keep a register. Old-fashioned but "does the trick." One of our traditions. Our quirks. There's no need to dwell on that moment of transition. What a wonderful bath you've had! Great! The stars and waters were aligned today. Your first day. You're here now. Be proud. I'd like to see some pride. No need to think about what brought you here, however cleansed it may currently be. There'll be time for that later. For now, this bed. This chair. Yes, a desk for journaling. But again, that later. For now, easy does it. There you go. Shhh. No tears. I don't want to have to call the attendants. Please don't make me have to do that. Off you go. Yes, lights out. I'm going now. We'll see you in the morning. You're fine. You're safe now. Just call if you need anything. We're always here for you. Yes, I'm going now. I'm going to XXXX the door behind you. Behind me. We won't use the "l" word here. You won't even hear the bolt moving into place.

Water, Rising

The bulbs in the sconces are dark, but I know my way. The portraits you collected from your co-exhibitionists follow my procession-of-one down the corridor, the eyes of their models concerned, skeptical. All of your own are now in storage. That is, if the warehouse bill has been paid. Among them, your life study of Golda. Golda and her portrait locked away. Modest Golda bared it all for you during those sessions, yet always maintained an aura of mystery. Fierce yet fragile. Present yet distant. I still remember our movie nights at the Thalia. Remember when we three saw *Hiroshima, Mon Amour* at the Thalia together? Remember the Thalia? Over Hungarian pastry afterward, you said that if things had been different, you might have proposed to her.

What would Golda say? That is, about what I see before me now. The wreckage of space. Or rather, its disintegration. I won't dwell. How does minimalism disintegrate? You never had much to begin with. Never wanted much. Except some acknowledgment, which you did receive, even if it flitted in and out. Seemed fleeting, insufficient, despite the years in the trenches. The gallery openings, the reviews you sometimes submitted. All the networking of which you were a master. The carefully-planted insights between brie and sesame cracker bites that determined a friend's career in art. Now, the once white walls have grown dusty, cobwebs intricate in corners. The droppings speak of fissures in walls and well-being. The dishes are unwashed, and indeterminate smells rise from sources equally indeterminate. Yes, that's mold I see on the multi-grain bread from the artisanal bakery down the block. My darling, I didn't know it had come to this.

There you go. Hush now. I'm here. Yes, you're awake. No, we aren't going to the hospital. We aren't going to speak of what might have been. Or the sham solutions ingested behind the gallery walls, the follow-up calls not made, that led to here. You're still here. I'm here now, even if I haven't always been. There's still time. Drape your arm around my neck, and we'll find a way to the shower. No worries, there's still soap in the bathroom closet. Yes, oatmeal & almond soap. Easy does it. Watch your step. Off with those drawers. Well, I'll get them off then. I've seen all this before, admittedly in a very different state. In a very different context. Years after your second solo show, when the fumblings became something else. An intimacy born of long knowledge. A different kind of love. Only we never replicated that night, even if our different kind of love remained. Even if I wasn't always steadfast, couldn't always be.

Bow your head. Let this water wash over you. I'm going to gently lather your back, your buttocks, between the cheeks. Now below your not-so privates. All of you. These are my arms around you. Feel my hands move in the here and now. Focus on the rhythm of their care. I, too, will focus so that I don't think about what might have been if you had let it be. If Golda had let it be. We will focus on this together-moment. Later, we will forage for food. There might still be something in the pantry. If not, I'll call for delivery. I won't leave you alone. And later still—for the sinew of the everyday. Now, we are here. Golda is, too—to make sure that you don't go the way she went. Now, we are together. Now, this ritual water. This oatmeal & almond soap. This rosemary and mint shampoo. Whatever spirits return from the past, they cannot remake the here.

Whatever arises to ensnarl the beyond, my darling, don't let the hygiene go.

Three's a Minyan

This building, our sanctuary, has seen better days.
Nights, too, sure enough.

The black and white tiles are worn into almost-ash.
Where did I once hear that marble is forever?

The floor is buckling.
The paint is cracking overhead.

Its flakes drift without hurry onto the grand chandelier,
confetti among crystals.

Here I was called into a manhood
I resisted, kicking and screaming

until my legs ached and my voice grew hoarse.
A manhood I still haven't found.

Here was the kiddush for the miracle of Malkah,
whose parents had so long hoped to welcome.

Outside, the needles litter the sidewalk.
The dealers and their customers negotiate in lethal embrace.

Some step away and rest on our benches.
Who would we be if we evicted them?

Their pleas—*please*—
mingle with our prayers.

Even the dollar store may soon be closing.
Such brazen theft, they say. Not even bothering to pilfer.

And still the nectar of the cantor's voice washes over me,
causing me to weep if I think about it

as he calls out the High Holiday liturgy
"*Hineni he-oni ....*"/Here I am, impoverished ...

In the ritual bath of that voice,
I am forgiven. Patched into crazy quilt.

And still we three assemble to honor what was
and what still is.

We see to it that the electric candles on each of the bimah's four posts
glow beneath their glass globes.

We ensure the suaveness of the prayerbook bindings.
We gather the page shards for burial.

And we gather to read the weekly Torah portion.
Instead of a single reader, we three take turns.

We will never surrender our Torah scrolls.
See their unstolen finials sparkle in this incandescent gloom.

We understand Jacob's devotion,
his love. We will wait, too.

We remember when one hundred was not unusual.
We remember when we hoped for ten.

Now we are content with, grateful for, three.
We mark the passage of days. And yes, again, the nights.

We stick with the texts, the songs.
The reminiscences on more recency/decency are in our blood,

our bones.
We won't rehash them.

Who are we?
We are three of fluidity tending a sliver of holiness.

We are three who shall not be moved.
We will stay until we are two or one.

Until our days are done.
Only let us not dwell there. But only here.

Though we are not ten,
we are still three.

We are neither patriarchs nor matriarchs.
We are without child. But children nonetheless.

Our prayers on that front were not answered.
That's sometimes how it is with prayers.

This building, our sanctuary, your sanctuary, sways amid the ruins.
We are the caretakers of this corner of supplication.

Come to us, child. You are welcome here.
Our melody flits and darts, gathers force as it rises,

east, and elsewhere,
somehow finding just the right key to open the gates of heaven.

Siesta's Sustenance

There's no narrative arc here. Instead, a framed vertical oval.
All that they taught us in literature class and

which I wrote down in my diligent if ungainly penmanship
in narrow-lined blue books had been imbibed

not in vain, but for another day.
Another hour. Other rooms.

Not the parlor, where tea is served on flower-bordered porcelain
to catch the latest gossip, and where newspapers crinkle in leisure.

Especially the book review section, often featuring Papa's
judicious, occasionally enthusiastic, offerings.

Although, to locate the arc, we really wouldn't have to look far.
We could always discuss the marriages, births, marriages, deaths…

stockpiled in Papa's lair all the way at the end of the hall,
mull the handwriting spidery over the pages somehow salvaged into exile.

We could consider the various certificates, charts, trees, and tomes
that led our family to this place of possibility at this moment in time.

But here, in these "front" rooms, the dénouement is missing;
the clash, the conflict, the climax, call it what you will,

if it exists, is utterly invisible.
Happens outside the frame, off the canvas.

No shouts here.
No broken plates. Or broken glass.

All I see are days delicate to discover. The intricacy of clues
that might be understood years later as ebbs and flows.

Mama passes on her culinary "secrets" to the neighborhood girls
whose mothers never mention her wish that I too had been born one.

Mama never teaches me these recipes, despite that wish,
although I eavesdropped from the gossamer of her closet.

And my nose remembers. Tagine. Paella. Shakshouka. Goulash.
The mélange that was Mama's "*Mangia*!"

They say the path to a man's heart is through his stomach.
Only Papa barely registers Mama's culinary alchemy;

so focused is he on her voice,
on the smoke and sway and swing of her.

The mezuzah wishes he would kiss *it* with such hunger.
Is Mama cooking for the neighborhood girls?

The breeze ruffles the lace curtains, vertical lines
interrupted by an idea of daisies that failed to interrupt the sun,

as Mama and Papa revel
in their so-called "siesta."

Omar calls to me.
Without his ever speaking,

without a pebble clinking on my bedroom window,
I know when he is waiting.

The pigeons make sure to deliver the unwritten message.
I descend to snuggle with Omar, to his body elongated,

his nipples breathtaking in the shadows, in the cacophony of secrecy,
to join him in a so-called "siesta" of our own.

M and M and the Queen Greet the S Queen

In honor of Miriam Isaacs

The stars are primping for their emergence. I almost want to say "debut," though they have done this time without count. Impossible to count. They know the drill, the dance. So yes, re-emergence, of course. But somehow always new. The peeking from the billows of the clouds' skirts. What could be construed as coquettish. But perhaps is shy. Apprehensive. Will the night, this night, welcome me?

Time to step away from the screen. The missives so urgent left to be answered. It's time. Queen, go to meet queen. Not, meet, but greet. You've met her so many times before. The queen of the day. No, the day that is queen. This sacred day. Down underground, cross the town, and then up way up above and there she almost is. Her veils are spreading across the taqueria. See to it that they don't get caught on the condiment tray or splattered with salsa verde.

Down into the valley she follows you to Miriam's place. Aaron Lebedeff smiles from the phonograph. The static—sound tinsel—catapults rhythm to my clunky-no-more feet. Up and down, all around. M is now reciting the blessings aloud in a way Mother never did. Mother reflective, silent, the Queen's touch feathery on her kerchief, dusting off the dandruff of weekday. Mother resplendent without weekday, anguish beckoning nearby.

M cuts the challah I bought from the market which I neglected to mention so different from the challah that Father once cut that Mother had kneaded separated challah braided polished baked in anticipation, in celebration, of the Queen's arrival. And then the soup and the kugel and the vegetables all so imaginatively prepared. The feast comes together. A bit of this, a pinch of that. Our foremothers knew how, too. This resourcefulness goes way—centuries—back.

M and I together, we are the hymn. This bounty, this fellowship, sings. The red envelopes unfurl their offerings. The spare room cinema framed by Yiddish literature is suddenly the setting of a poultry plant where *all* of the male chicks are killed. Unlike the *makat bekhorot*, the plague against the firstborn. Of course, there's a justification for this (unritual) slaughter, and it all makes financial "sense." Still the chicks are slaughtered. How can it be called “sexing”? Is this a variant of the eros/Thanatos connection?

Only there is much else to focus onscreen beside the carnage. It’s only a blip of a plot catalyst, right? And there are also nuts—cashews—on hand. Do birds eat cashews? And if it weren’t for this particular red envelope offering, with its rumination on the aftermath of “sexing,” there would be another. Until the red envelopes are no more, of course. Their fan retreats, crumpled into oblivion.

But for now, this is our time-out from time marching on. And a new Sabbath. A secular Sabbath. A spiritual Sabbath. For the Queen does not forsake us. She, too, is a cinephile. A fan of friendship. She has her opinions. Four stars below the heavens? Five stars? Let the critics pontificate. The Queen never divulges. The Queen merely smiles mysteriously.

No matter. The stars overhead, outside, are twinkling now. Ensconced. Set in their ways. Again, they know what to do. The Queen takes Mother’s arm. Has Mother been here all along? Yes. Watching (with) us? Yes. Yes, of course. I follow the Queen’s ghostly train and Mother’s varicose veins down to the train. Mother’s face flickers against the metro tunnel’s walls, only partially obscured by the Queen’s still-white veil.

(Not Entirely) New World Rituals

The woman answering the phone knows my voice, can anticipate my request. And yet I make no effort to change that request in any way, to step away from the well-worn path. Still, with a pause, gentle, almost tender, in its solicitousness, she waits for me to say: "One steamed veggie egg roll and steamed tofu with mixed veggies and brown rice." Without ever having studied the choreography or even so much as glanced at the libretto, each of us knows the steps prescribed to us in this dance, this bonsai waltz. We never glide outside the white-scalding lines. We never introduce ourselves. We never step past the briefest of pleasantries. We cannot. We must not. We wouldn't dare.

And when I enter from my "journey" from down the street, she waves at me from the back, as her son (?), now a young man after these many years, completes the transaction up front. On my return home from her establishment (or at least the one where she answers the phone), I think I vow that I will try something different, fare from another place, another culture. I think to myself: "It's not Christmas day, after all, and I won't be going to the cinema." Why shouldn't I voyage forth to other shores?

Only I head upstairs. From the cupboard, I remove the stoneware plate decorated with an orange and red rooster gifted to me by a friend who joined the Hare Krishnas. Slice of a set that never fails to provide cheer. Just as its donor once never failed to, either. Carefully, I remove the veggie egg roll from the wax paper. I scoop out the brown rice from the white carboard container onto which a red structure has been printed. A house? A temple? Though not manna from the heavens, I savor each mouthful. Instead of leftover *tsholnt* or gefilte fish, here is this sustenance that no longer elicits surprise yet remains only partially known. Conceived from afar, created here. Cherished here, too.

What were the steps that brought us both, her and me, to this street that never quite "turns the corner"? I'll never know. Even my own path, let alone hers. I place the paper materials carefully in the recycling bag. Without a road map, without a specific blessing such as the ones I used to recite with full intent, such as the ones whose laws I had to memorize for *berakhot*/ blessing bees, there is a ritual to this practice. In the way I make sure every grain of brown rice is eaten. This is the fruit of the determination of the voyagers, the uprooted, the displaced, and the generations that follow. It has to be.

Even as I phrase my question, I have learned to step away from answers. The signposts flash by, but my eyes look down, focusing on the water now running down into the mounds of soap suds. I won't register for the genealogists' convention. The water is turning cold. The yellow dishwasher gloves flash unused from the left-hand corner of the counter. I dry the plate with the orange and red rooster, and my hands, crimson from the water, violet with trepidation, face the new week ahead. The red structure creaks under the weight of my night. One of its roof tiles loosens beneath the gales of my breath.

Her voice will light the way.

Unanswered Questions Around the Endemic Bend

Beneath the transparent shield, the white awning lowered over much of his already-ghostly face gleams in the post-dawn light, a beacon of a sort. But what is the message of its call? Whom is it reaching? No one seems available to witness, to see it as such or at all. They look down or altogether away, not blinded, but shielding their eyes in sleepiness or indifference or perhaps not having noticed at all. And why shouldn't they? This—the specter/spectacle of him—isn't a sight new to them. The faces of a few are themselves similarly clad. What is there to say that can be said in a flash on a nearly-empty sidewalk or on a commuter train? What is there to say that cannot be better and otherwise said? In the faces of the bereaved. The tales of the too-soon dead never told. In the unavailability of the funeral parlors. In the fatigue and warnings of the medical professionals. In the statistical reports that haven't been shelved or buried.

In the laughs as he walked by. In the scorn hissed: "It won't protect you!" or "It doesn't do anything!" Words he ignored. Or rather, ones to which he did not respond. A lifetime of having scorn heaped upon him has prepared him for such moments. Their taunts get absorbed in the cloth. He can taste their residue. The smolder of their still burning ashes. Their red-gray. Their scald. The residue of fire unextinguished. At least, there are no fists. At least, he doesn't find himself shoved to the pavement. So that's something. Had an earlier era when the news of the sick and dying rendered him differently immobile prepared him for this? Perhaps. Perhaps not. Those particles were transferred in such a specific way. These here are so much more plentiful. Both ubiquitous and cunning. Still, the process of shielding—walling—isn't unfamiliar. He's no stranger to quarantine, not only of the body, but of the spirit.

The bodies press against him. Into him. The rush hour commute hasn't thinned through the years, despite the dire predictions and notices of office buildings abandoned in the city's center. He checks again. In this corner of the train, no one is similarly enveloped. Still only a few coverings dot the landscape. Little has changed since he first boarded. He scans for a corner where he might be less surrounded. Closer to a door. Closer to escape from the invisible enemy. Even those close to him (beyond this train) tell him he must get out more. Life is passing him by. They are concerned. Well, actually, they are worried. This (whatever it is) isn't healthy. He must get out. Again, beyond this train, that is. To the cinema, to the concert hall, to gallery openings, to lectures. He has to mingle. *Only connect!* The garret isn't the answer. Under the guise of the public health crisis, or rather now, the vestiges of the crisis, he is caught in the complacency of an older self. Trapped in the comfort of a well-worn housecoat. He hears coughing next to him. Tries to dodge its waves. Its fluorescent comets exploding and crashing.

Finally, he disembarks, transitions into the final stage of his commute. Following the closing of the train door, questions crowd around him. Was he able to dodge the particles? Will this be the time he succumbed? Did the boosters boost … or will they leave him in the lurch? And then the foundational questions that never leave, even when he is "safely" ensconced in the garret: Who will care for me if I fall? If I cannot rise? If the particles fell me, who will help me down the hall and across the white tiles?
Through the tenacious tangled tunnel of fog, who will tend me?

האַר, האַרץ, ווי אַזוי וועל איך וויסן אַז איך בין פֿרײַ?

Har, harts, vi azoy vel ikh visn az ikh bin fray?

God, beloved, how will I know that I am free?

Object Lessons/Treasure, Retained

I.

The mirror doesn't lie, it is said.
Even in the pre-dusk light further bleached by the leaves of the shade trees
and the tangle of the scrub brush encroaching upon the garret,
it announces its truth without guile or subterfuge.
With a kind of hard, feral charisma.
A tussle that compels,
even if it will be a losing one
for the figure facing the silvered glass.

And so he has learned to avoid its siren call.
He won't be drawn into that ritual examination
that used to take up so much of his time
all those decades ago,
that erupted into sirens behind his tired eyes.
The dots from the removal of hairs
that should have remained on the locations of the body
where they had been seeded.

The flagellation over the pizza that should never been snarfed.
The yearning for shoulders to be bigger,
for a waist to be smaller,
for arms to be more sculpted,
for a cock to be thicker,
for the body to be … well, taller,
closer to the uppermost cupboard shelves or the trees
or the silver of the heavens themselves.

Closer to the realm of the idolized.
The wish list that was never quite fulfilled,
despite the years of effort
in the temples of vigor
and the years of prayer,
the lying prostrate before the idols of the flesh
and the spirit who remained indifferent.
The sessions of demons, determination, and despair.

II.

Now, as he returns from the third medical appointment of the week,
as this and that body part demands tending,
teeters,
as this chronic condition (he hates to use the word "disease")
and its required treatment set in motion
not unexpected but still terrifying aftereffects,
require ever more contorted sets of pirouetting
to manage, to navigate,

he remembers those earlier sessions before the mirror.
The endless navel loathing,
the insistence upon inadequacy,
the refusal to accept the temple
that is the gift granted by God
for a brief period in the history of time until it returns to dust.
Now, what he would do to be transported back to that earlier body!
Only there is no going back.

And there is no looking back.
From emotional wreckage,
now this on-the-brink-of wreck.
This is the current state of things.
He will not seek out the mirror.
But neither will he avert his gaze.
And he certainly won't give it away,
even as he knows there would be takers.

For its frame is sturdy.
Uncarved,
but well varnished.
The maker's label and its location
—Rochester, N.Y.—
is still on the back.
He must have unearthed it on one of his thrift shop
or yard sale expeditions.

It does well in the bedroom.
Expands the space.
Animates the epochs beyond, the ghosts within, the garret walls.
And so it will stay,
glittering in pre-dusk and other light,
a talisman of so much energy perhaps not completely squandered, but
mis-focused,
of life lessons battering the gossamer of autumn dreamscape,
and as a hand of years remaining extended in overture and invitation.

What the Babushkas Saw

Why did we not speak often of Evgeny?

Now that we're filing into his chamber,
we are engulfed by the history of our silence/s
(or perhaps the weight of our terror).
Our shoes clamber on the unhappy floorboards.
Should we have removed them?
The old woman who let us in said we could keep them on.
Who was she to grant permission?
Neighbor? Superintendent? Janitor? Busybody?
The heaviness of our trudging resounds
like a slow-moving herd of massive land animals,
sounds even more lugubrious than the final shovel hitting earth,
than clods of dirt hitting a coffin.
Not that we would know in this case, or case history, as it were.
What lumps we are. Clods indeed.

Why did we not speak (more) often of Evgeny?

Now that we've lowered ourselves onto the bed, the few chairs, the floor,
we don't speak at all. We can't find the words.
We don't know what to do with our hands.
We hide them in our pockets or beneath us.
We stare at the half-moons of our fingernails,
the ones which have not been torn out.
We gaze at the unadorned walls.
Have the pictures been removed?
Perhaps there never were any.
A few of us step closer to examine the strata of blankness.
What color is all of this? Gray? Brown? Of course, not ochre.
Taupe? Ah yes, taupe.
Anything but to consider he who once dwelled here, among us.
An occasional cough or sneeze interrupts the density of our stasis.

Why did we not speak of Evgeny?

It wasn't so long ago that he was speaking with us.
The lawns undulated lush and freshly mowed behind him—
and beneath the pirouetting of our bare feet.

The lake shimmered in the light of not yet dusk;
its surface unbroken save for the water fowl traveling across it.
We swore that the green of the lawns
surpassed even the green of the ducks' heads in brilliance.
Sipping Evgeny's grandmother's blueberry wine,
such insistences were what mattered to us in those days, those weeks.
Evgeny's grandmother appeared at a front window of her dacha,
her brow below her kerchief furrowed even in the glitter of that grove.
The pines, as resolute and towering as they were, could not dislodge
Evgeny's grandmother from the black frame,
the white trim, of her unease.

Only Evgeny was not to be deterred.
He stepped forward from the froth of our patter
into a clearing, with the sun, even in its ebbing state, his spotlight.
There, he read poems from the almost-national poet,
in his own translation into the minority language.
No one had known that he knew the minority language,
much less that he could translate into it.
Perhaps he had poems of his own in that language, too.
How could a vehicle so charming be so supple, so revolutionary,
we wondered in the delicious torpor of the blueberry wine.
Even the preoccupation of those poems—
the campaign to construct a grid of courage,
the invocation for the return of nightingale song—
could not penetrate the wine's hold.

Why do we not speak of Evgeny?

Even now, even here, in this impromptu assemblage
Convened not by handbill or broadside or announcement or invitation,
or even by word of mouth,
but by the force of the sun's blackness,
by the impending blue of the half-moon,
by the indecorous stationing of the stars,
by the careening of the constellations,
by bones landed we know not where,
by words recited on the banks of a late summer lake
that had hushed we who could not stop talking,

even now, even here, we dare not speak his name.
We find no gesture to reshape the din of this quiet.
We will not pack away his things.
Let the old woman of indeterminate authority handle that.

Instead, we remember Evgeny's recitation,
the smiles and murmurs that greeted its completion.
We remember the gathering of goblets
and the emptied crystal decanter,
the folding of blankets—
how its plaid squares were aligned, how its flowers flowed into garlands.
We remember the eyes of Evgeny's grandmother drilling into us
as we made our way into whatever careless, pointedly casual
sleeping configuration we had prearranged or fallen into.
Now, we rise. We sneak an irrevocable glimpse of Evgeny's place of
never-rest
and file down the stairs in our stockinged feet.
We wonder if the old woman is watching us from her room
and if she has alerted others in this city of unlit street lamps
of our visit—our last pilgrimage—to Evgeny.

A Summons in Spring

The driveway was long but not winding. Direct, blunt even. The front gate locked but easily scalable. Dusted, not caked, with rust. Paint chipped. The young and not-so-young-but-still spry found their way through its pliant bars. The cameras were still on but no one checked the video. Who had time? Everyone knew about the museum. There had been talk some time ago of turning the building into artist studios. Or was it condos? Yes, that must have been it. The meetings had been well-attended and surprisingly calm. He hadn't attended the meetings, remembers them only as a long-ago item in the metro section.

Still, he felt himself pulled. Summoned, really. At dusk, the pines whispered his name. Gently, but repeatedly. He had a way with pines, or rather, pines had a way with him. Always had. Only these were different. They spoke with certainty, conveyed urgency. The coyotes were even more dogged (!), barking insistently their invitation.

It was on one March moment, on his evening constitutional, when hands—speckled with brown spots, yet strong—forcefully ushered him through the gates and up that aforementioned long, blunt, unwinding drive. Given the calls of the pines and the coyotes, he wasn't surprised. In fact, he'd been expecting them, those hands. This descent, this convergence, of hands. Rows of remnants of daffodils swayed in the stillness. He found himself before a burnt-red brick edifice interrupted by tall and narrow, unbroken, windows.

And then without knowing how, he was inside. Had he been whisked, or, as earlier, guided? Before him gleamed vitrine after vitrine filled with dolls. Elegantly clad, perfectly coiffed tresses gleaming behind the glass. Bisque faces unmarred by the spanking of Father Time. Eyes that followed him with alertness. He knew he was not their first visitor, and that they could fend for themselves. From so many cultures, time periods, places. And yet there were no object labels. Why had the object labels been taken but the dolls left here, "unharmed"? And so he wasn't really sure what he was seeing or from whence they had come. Slovenian native costume? Crafted by whose hands? From which famed dollmaker down which narrow, cobbled lane, third door from which firefighters' communal dining hall? Or by a machine—he could hear their clatter, see the racing of hands to avoid hungry blades, the pursed lips of the supervisor—in a building long shuttered or razed.

Why were they all still here? Perhaps they'd refused to be moved. After all, dolls had power. Wasn't that really the reason that Father had cut off Midge's nose so long ago? Or was it because dolls are a representation of the human form and therefore potentially worshipped as idols? And little boy he had so adored Midge. Yes, worshipped even, if it must be known. Father's maiming of her had sent him into paroxysms of undammable tears, waves of weeping that racked his body for hours, sapped his spirit for months. Decades. How dare Father maim Midge?

His own adoration of Midge was different from his worship of Barbie and her friends alongside her. Yes, he'd worshipped Barbie, too. Wanted to be her. To join her confident, never coy, social set. Yearned for her silent, eternal poise; her buxom yet lithe form. Unfazed by catcalls, gravity, the constriction of social mores. Yet it was Midge that Father had gotten hold of. Barbie and the others had managed to elude the tentacles of his originalist interpretation of the law. Or hardline custom, he really wasn't sure. Barbie and her friends tried to warn Midge in that secret language of dolls, to make her aware of the danger, but Midge, anchored in the certainty of her youthful charms, thought she knew better, thought she could escape. Only she was no match for Father's determination. He would have warned her, only he hadn't known. How could he? He was no legal scholar. He had daydreamed his way through Talmud class. Barely hanging on, if you must know.

After the mutilation, the wreckage, after the shattering of his naiveté, he caressed Midge, swore his own eternal allegiance to her. He would take better care. Midge only stared at him blankly, coolly even, in the face of his blather. What could words like "take better care" possibly mean to her now?

These dolls now encased in vitrines before him, he realized, had strength in assemblage. For all the delicacy of their features, limbs, and costume, they would never allow what had happened to Midge to happen to them. They would not allow themselves to be touched, let alone removed. The funding may have run out; the health of their home was at stake. And yet, the glass of the vitrines had been freshly polished. So too the marble floors.

He glided through the echoless exhibition halls in search of Midge. Of course, she wasn't here. Couldn't possibly be. Had no place among these costumed bisque "baby/little girl" dolls. Still, he looked carefully at every vitrine in all of the many halls. He was sure that dolls here would agree that Midge could find a place here. After all, Midge wasn't really all that different in age from these dolls. He was sure these dolls, with their demonstrated staying power, would not have allowed the maiming of Midge. If only Midge could have been brought here, even if only temporarily. If only he had known of this place when he was a five-year old, he could have brought Midge here. Here, Midge would have remained whole.

When the sun was beginning to imagine its own ascent, he felt hands—the very ones that has brought about his entry—now, yes, whisking, him out, down the drive, through the gate. The pines were quiet. If not altogether gone, the coyotes were quieter, too. He could still hear their whining.

But high above all, he could hear the keen of wailing. It wasn't coming from the Barbie and her set of memory. No, it was coming from the museum. From the rotunda at the building's center, beneath the skylight, where there were no dolls at all. A chorus in lament. He wouldn't allow himself to look, to investigate. He wouldn't try to parse the strands of lament. But he could hear Midge. He'd know her voice anywhere. Midge was unforgotten.

Midge was finally weeping.

Plain Plenty: Blossom, Bounty, Betty

After the pinks and whites, the blossoms,
which should not be skipped over,
for, instead of a truncated overture,
they deserve a poem of their own.
A proper poem.
For a different time…

So let me begin again:
After the pinks and whites,
these delicate marvels.
Such round. Such red.
Or green or gold.
So many colors.

So many forms. So many types.
Always recognizable. Always connected.
Familial, you know.
Such spare sweetness.
Serene.
So ready in autumn. Sometimes earlier.

The birds and the bees
and the bugs
… and the worms … agree.
They want in on the bounty.
So too the roan mare outside.
Don't forget to cut it into pieces for her.

And, too, the neighbor's donkey.
He deserves one, as well.
A treat.
A break from hay and oats.
Work horse?
Work donkey!

Dazzle on tree.
Brightness between branches.
Perfect in a wooden bowl on Lavinia's kitchen table.
Or on a white earthenware plate next to tea. No scones needed.

Snap. Snap. Crunch. Crunch.
The juices seep into the skin's pores. And the soul's.

Or into the crisps and crumbles and pies and tarts and Betty's.
Are you partial to the flour
and (aforementioned) oats of crisp
or the breadcrumbs atop Betty?
Is that cinnamon and butter and cloves I smell in the oven?
Maybe ginger?

But I digress
for those are not the stars of this poem.
Those are the enhancements.
Nor is its butter that is spread over wheat toast,
the very butter you purchased one October
(instead of a t-shirt) at a mountainside visitors center.

So adaptable.
May you continue to flourish in so many climates.
May there yet be winter for your contentment.
Flee you from the crisis.
Here's a map of an unpolluted world.
May your blossoms breathe in the time they need and are needed.

While others herald the charms of brighter colors,
gather in the bogs for the tangy ones,
fly to warmer zones for neon results,
we sing of humble.
Fruit not bitter.
Fruit not strange.

Blessed be the orchardist.
Blessed be the pickers,
be they arrived from far or near.
Sustain them in harmony
and safety, far from the coyotes' net.
Provide them a thriving wage.

Today, the sun is mild.
Today, the air is redolent.
Today we will go harvesting in the back yard.
Today, we will go further afield.
Into the fields.
Said the guide:

Walk the country road until you reach the sunflowers.
Turn left.
If you focus, you will find it.
Follow the footsteps of this faint perfume.
Open the creaking gate.
I know it needs to be oiled.

Walk some fifty paces.
And there you are.
And there they are.
Without fanfare, without trumpets,
the miracle of manna in the desert.
The icebox thrums in anticipation.

Ignorance, Bliss

I walk along an autumnal country road.
Eventually, there will be a fork,
and of course, I will have to make a decision.
But for now, there are these reverberations.
Ones I cannot identify.
Although I suppose with today's gadgets,
I could find a way to do so. Only I do not.

Is that a caw?
And that other—the howl of a coyote?
What of this crooning buzz that seems
to be emerging from the brush alongside the creek
now low from lack of rainfall?
Or is it coming from the creek itself?
When will the rains come?

Here, bales of hay are lined up against the horizon's line;
there, they dot the fields.
A low stone wall marks a crucial boundary
whose meaning I will never know.
This is not the time to envision disputes
or hours spent in courtrooms
or feuds long-lasting that occasionally erupt into the summoning of police.

Far off in a distance, a structure of some sort
is barely visible through the trees I know are not evergreens,
but whose identities escape me. I smile at the proverbial kindness
        of these strangers.
The structure could be a house or a shed or a romantic getaway.
Perhaps young lovers sneak off there now to perform paradise
        in the now almost-ruin.
Perhaps not.
As you can tell, the intentions of its builders and its possible
        denizens elude me.

Horses neigh in the distance.
I wonder what color their coats are
and whether they've had a good day grazing.
A rooster crows repeatedly. Urgently, I imagine.

But what do I know of rooster calls?
I picture his beard jiggling.
What danger does he sense that causes this late-hour crowing?

For all my gliding, my footsteps echo on the asphalt.
An occasional truck roars by.
Or so it seems to me,
given the stillness of the road, the time of day.
And the unjangle of my nerves.
The sky is saturated with streaks of rose and gold and flame.
A clash that is the custom, a conflagration in harmony.

I cannot locate the borders of each color,
but they are all there.
Each as was intended. Here, that—if perhaps only that—I know.
Against this panorama,
and through this choir concert of unknown,
past and present, I reciprocate the unhesitant embrace of
the beginning of the close of day.

Flaneur of the Fields

Thus, I bent over a suitcase excavated from the thrift shop
a few blocks down from the Graham Avenue subway stop
one with snaps and milky cappuccino exterior and mustiness within
that might once have set sail to
Dubrovnik or Marseilles or Andorra
only there were no stickers on the outside only their outlines
so I was left to speculate on the scrimping so long for getaways
for visas on vistas beheld and remembered

in search of an ensemble
suitable for celebrating this farmland now fallow
recovering as I myself so yearned to do
for walking the hills rolling gently
past these venerable plate-glass windows
without discernible trails of any kind
but replete with rocks
and twists and dips unforeseen

one to cloak this form in middle age's twilight
with its newfound bulges and deflations
something practical and if not outrageous then sassy
that would not emphasize but also would not conceal
gray turtleneck black flannels below
knitted black cardigan topped by orange scarf
yes sure
for orange is the new old goes with gray

and what need
had I now
of tendrils of smoke
and declamation
and Dadaist
happening
in absinthe-filled
café

and I did walk out to the back porch and the mare and her foal
so exuberant fresh to the world stood in the distance
but the feral cat came close curious about

and dare I say admiring of my sartorial splendor
and spread her scent glands across the bottoms of my flannels
marking me as hers and I buried my face in her streaked fur
in the generous rumbling that was Lucy
so grateful was I for her understanding and ownership

and with her encouragement
I ventured beyond the farmyard and into the fields
with their heavens and pines and grasses and rolls of hay
as inscrutable purveyors of my solo runway show
that was without applause
the feral cat having departed the audience
my insistence on the possibility of
fashion without other eyes probing in assessment

and I was grateful for having arrived
at this moment of
if not recovery
then rest
and I knew that I would
somehow
some way
go on

toward the bounty of the shade tree
extended along the horizon
whose long fingers
with their
trilling
tickling
fondling
whispering of light

would lead me
fortified by my shabby suitcase
bulging with signifiers of dapperdom and determination
and by the residue from Lucy's whiskers
deeper into the fields whose very green
would camouflage then dim however briefly

the unacknowledged abyss   the green gleam
of my grief

College Grove, Tennessee, October 15, 2023

Hole(s) in the Walls/Shelter Island

There are no granite countertops here. Nor quartz ones. No stainless-steel appliances. The cabinets have not been retouched since ... Nor is there much in the way of vintage charm. No crown molding. No wainscoting. No built-ins. No glass doorknobs. No stained glass windows. No beveled or leaded ones, either, for that matter. No original glass at all. The bathroom, with its plastic wrap-around tub and walls, the absence of wall tile, has been written about elsewhere. Mice scurry in and out of the openings above the floorboards, the holes in the walls. Would steel wool suffice? Fat chance. Or skinny one. Old, worn, shabby, run-down, take your pick—yes. Charming? Filled with "character"? Not at all. Even if the apps make it a point not to herald absence, it is crucial that you are aware of this list, this collection of lack. This much no.

And that's just inside. Outside, a rusting chain metal fences topped by barbed wire separates this building from an ever-encroaching undefined wasteland. A mid-sized green plastic ball for an indeterminate sport (kickball?) is stuck deflated in the underbrush. Will anyone ever come to claim it? Do balls disintegrate? Ivy aggressively chokes the trees whose branches extend close to the windows. What chance stand these trunks? How much longer can they withstand the chokehold of the ivy and the growing gusts of the climate crisis? Against other trees flourish long ropes of green-brownery, as if towers of Komondor dogs or ghosts of Rapunzels past are proliferating upright here and now in this particular patch of wasteland. The bushy tail of a squirrel droops listlessly in the orange, smoke-from-Canada air, even as one of its ears remains cocked towards the heated discussion on Yiddish avant-garde poetry taking place on Zoom only a few feet away.

As the planet's health grows ever more fragile, as the word "freedom" is blasted with greater frequency, precisely as it is applied to a few and ripped away from the many, as the orange haze blanketing the nation and the world grows ever more scalding, as the plague's variants multiply and grow ever more cunning, as new plagues loom threateningly from zombieland, so I cling, kicking and screaming, to these unimpressive walls. These ones without the "wow" factor, without curb appeal, for whom something visionary, something epically far-reaching, will have to be done to achieve resale. On these worn, scratched floor boards, my body takes steps, anchored in the work yet to be done that edges beyond the known into the cosmos.

Even without plants, there is photosynthesis. Photos, from the recent and distant past, are synthesized into consciousness. Here is Mother walking with us after a supper of fish cakes and green beans. Here are sister and I playing with Sharon and Janelle from a few houses down. On their porch. Did we ever dare go inside their house? Hopscotch, yes. Jump rope, yes. Here, too, Montaigne's *Selected Essays* in the translation by John Florio edited and with an introduction by Lester G. Crocker. There is no time here to elaborate on their power. You who know already know. You who do not may yet soon. The walls, the so-called "unimpressive" walls are not indifferent to this designation of mine. But they take a longer view.

After all, how much longer will I be here? And given the wasteland's march, how long will the building itself endure before the ground beneath is reclaimed by a force not as yet nameable, or even known. The walls have ears, they say. Eyes, too. Boring into the nucleus of light. And footsteps. Of the squirrels of today … and the ghosts of inhabitants past. I hear them some nights. Not tonight, though. Not on this night of *doikayt*, of hereness. I turn off the lamp, make my way to the bed that knows the shapes of these limbs. Constellations illuminate the vast expanse of that micro- journey across this expanse of carpetlessness. The city quiets, even if it doesn't cease, its humming. The walls of the garret sigh. Not in frustration, I maintain, as I glimpse the first harbingers of sleep. But in contentment. When I reach frantically for the tendrils of sleep that I detect in the distance, I hear the squirrels chuckling at my hubris.

At Last, a Celebration, or,
Improvisations on the Question of Inspiration

When I go,
don't tear your clothes,
and don't wear black,
don't conceal your mirrors,
don't sit on the floor,
don't avoid the shower,
don't recite the Kaddish,
don't speak in hushed tones.
Don't mourn at all.

When I go,
have a party.
Let there be flowers bright and tumultuous.
Let there be cheese, crackers, wine, fruit, humus,
cookies, milk chocolates, gelato, sparkling pear cider.
Whatever you'd like.
Whatever is decadent, inappropriate.
In commemoration, let this day be a day without diet.
Bring your dog. Feed her non-scraps from the table of bounty.

When I go,
convene some viewing parties. Maybe for:
A Room With A View,
Beasts of the Southern Wild,
Nights of Cabiria,
Jules et Jim,
Daughters of the Dust.
Anything by Satyajit Ray.
Anything with Judy Holliday.

When I go,
play the music at high volume.
Invite the neighbors.
Nothing by Samuel Barber or Henryck Górecki or Arvo Pärt.
Maybe something by Lucinda Williams or the Communards.
Or Louis Armstrong or the B-52's. Or Benny Goodman.
Something you can dance to. Let that inner dervish sparkle.

.

Something that gets you swiveling
From on high, from my freshly-dug new eternal home, I need to see
you gyrate.

When I go,
read aloud, to each other, or alone,
not Bible verses or pieties from the sages, but poems.
Maybe something by Nina Cassian or Rosario Castellanos.
Maybe Frank O'Hara, Tim Dlugos, Thom Gunn, Essex Hemphill.
Maybe Minnie Bruce Pratt or Irena Klepfisz or Rokhl Korn.
Or Jane Kenyon, Lucille Clifton, Anne Sexton.
Read poets I've never heard of.
Read poems you think I would have liked.

When I go,
take a hike.
Walk to the mountains.
Listen to the quiet's thrum.
Stand with your arms
outspread in the rain.
Look into the eyes of the fox unexpected at your November picnic.
Lie down in a field of wild grasses
despite the slyness of sun.

When I go,
Celebrate as was never done in my life,
during which birthdays were not celebrated,
nor a wedding ever made.
Make some noise.
Wear your most festive outfit. Something revealing.
Play it bacchanalian.
Let there be no heads shaken in pity.
Tears are acceptable, but only those of joy.

And afterwards,
take the leftovers home with you.
Distribute them to the homeless woman on the street. Place them in
her hands.
Resist. You'll know what.
Kiss your beloved in abandon.
Caress unexpected places.
Remember our late dinners in the diner on the square
after the rallies.
Remember the baritone notes of this cappuccino as it banishes
our hangover.
Heed a life lived on the margins, without heirs
or ties of blood or oath.

Practice delight. Rejoice!

און נאָך דעם,
נעם אַהיים די שיריים.
גיט זיי דער היימלאָזער פֿרוי אויף דער גאַס. שטעל זיי אין אירע הענט.
שטעל זיך אַנטקעגן. דו וועסט וויסן וואָס.
קוש דײַן געליבטע מיט הפֿקירות.
גלעט אומדערוואַרטעטע ערטער.
געדענק אונדזערע שפּעט-נאַכטיקע וועטשערעס אינעם
    רעסטאָראַן אויפֿן סקווער נאָך די מיטינגען.
געדענק די באַריטאָנע טענער פֿון אָט דעם קאַפּוטשינוֹ בשעת
    ער טרײַבט אַוועק דײַן קאַצן-יאָמער.
רעכען זיך מיט אַ לעבן געלעבט אויף די ראַנדן, אָן יורשים אָדער
    באַציונגען פֿון בלוט אָדער שבֿועה.

מאַכט פֿרייד. פֿריי זיך!

עפּעס אַרומצודרייען זיך.
פֿון אויבן אָן, פֿון דער נאָר-וואָס געגראָבטע נײַ-אייביק היים דאַרף איך קוקן
אויף דיר וויגן מיט די היפּטן.

ווען איך גיי אַוועק לייען פֿאַר,
איינער צום אנדערן, אָדער אַליין,
ניט קיין פסוקים, ניט קיין פֿרומקייטן פֿון די צדיקים, נאָר לידער.
אפֿשר: עפּעס פֿון נינאַ קאַסיאַן, ראָזאַריאָ קאַסטעיאַנאָס,
אפֿשר פֿרענק או' האַראַ, טים דלוגאָס, טהאָם גאַן, עסעקס העמפּהילל.
אפֿשר מיני ברוס פּרעט אָדער אירענאַ קלעפּפֿיש אָדער רחל קאָרן.
אָדער אפֿשר דזשיין קעניאָן, לוסיל קליפֿטאָן, אַנן סעקסטאָן.
לייען פֿאַר פּאָעטן וואָס איך האָב קיין מאָל ניט געוווּסט.
לייען פֿאַר לידער וואָס דו מיינסט וואָלטן מיך געפֿאַלן.

ווען איך גיי אַוועק,
גיי אויף אַ שפּאַציר.
גיי אין די בערג.
הער זיך צו אויף דער שטילקייט.
שטיי מיט די אָרעמס
אויסגעשפּרייט אינעם רעגן.
קוק אַרײַן אין די אויגן פֿונעם פֿוקס ניט-דערוואַרטן בײַ דײַן נאָוועמבער-פּיקניק.
לייג זיך אַוועק אין אַ פֿעלד פֿון ווילדע גראָזן
כאַטש דעם געביפּטקייט פֿון זון.

ווען איך גיי אַוועק,
פֿריי זיך ווי עס איז קיין מאָל ניט געטאָן אין מײַן לעבן,
ווען געבוירן-טעג זײַנען קיין מאָל ניט געפּראַוועט געוועןֿ,
און אַ חתונה קיין מאָל ניט געמאַכט.
מאַך רעש.
טו אָן דײַן יום-טובֿדיקסטער גאַרניטער. עפּעס אין וואָס מע קען זען אַ ביסל הויט.
שפּיל עס סעקסי.
זאָל ניט זײַן קיין קעפּ געשאָקלט אין רחמנות.
טרערן מעל מען אָננעמען, אָבער נאָר טרערן פֿון פֿרייד.

צום סוף, אַ פֿײַערונג,
אָדער אימפּראָוויזאַציעס אויף דער פֿראַגע פֿון אינספּיראַציע

ווען איך גיי אַוועק,
רייס ניט די קליידער,
און טראָג ניט קיין שוואַרץ,
באַהאַלט ניט דעם שפּיגל,
זעץ זיך ניט אויפֿן דיל,
מײַד ניט אויס דעם שפּריץ,
זאָג ניט דעם קדיש,
רעד ניט אין ווייכע שטימען.
זײַ ניט קיין אָבֿל אין גאַנצן.

ווען איך גיי אַוועק,
מאַך פֿאַר זיך אַ שׂימחה.
לאָז זײַן בלומען, העלע און טומלדיקע.
לאָז זײַן קעז, פּלעצלעך, ווײַן, פֿרוכט, חומוס,
קיכלעך, מילך-שוקולאַדן, דזשעלאַטאָ, גלאַנצנדיק באַרזאַפֿט.
וואָס דו ווילסט.
אַלץ וואָס איז דעקאַדענט, אַלץ וואָס פּאַסט ניט.
לכּבֿוד דעם אָנדענק האַלט ניט די דיעטע.
ברענג דײַן הונט מיט. גיט זי צו עסן די ניט-ברעקלעך פֿונעם טיש פֿון שפֿע.

ווען איך גיי אַוועק,
פֿאַרזאַמלט אַ ווײַזונג-מסיבה. אפֿשר צו זען:
אַ צימער מיט אַן אויסבליק,
חיות פֿונעם דרומדיקן ווילדערניש,
נעכט פֿון קאַביריאַ,
דזשול איי דזשים,
טעכטער פֿונעם שטויב.
אַבי וואָס פֿון סאַטיאַדזשיט ריי.
אַבי וואָס מיט דזשודי האָלידיי.

ווען איך גיי אַוועק,
שפּיל הויך די מוזיק.
פֿאַרבעט די שכנים.
גאָרניט פֿון סאַמועל באַרבער אָדער הענריק גורעצקי אָדער אַרוואָ פּיירט.
אפֿשר עפּעס פֿון לוסינדאַ וויליאַמס אָדער די קאָמונאַרדס.
אָדער לואי אַרמסטראָנג אָדער די בי-52'ס. אָדער בעני גודמאַן.
עפּעס מיטצוטאַנצן. לאָז גלאַנצן דעם אינערלעכן דערוויש.

Along the Path of Peppermint Pillows: Notes to My Readers

Night Breaks in the Garret is a meditation not so much on the search for home, but rather, on the coming to terms with what is, here and now, home. The physical space of home, as well as its historical roots and emotional and psychological implications, are central to the narrative arc of the text. Home in place, in situ. Home in and out (mostly out) of a faith community. Once home, always foundational. Living in the fertile space of its borderlands. Visit, flee, return, peek. Flee again. Breathe. Intermittent exodus. Language as homeland, no, as borderland. Moving between languages. One more of a home if home means comfort, sureness of step across the rope bridge swaying over the swollen, post-storm river. Never fully certain in the other tongue, the second, or rather, the third, imbibed. But still so much love, so much whispering from between the babka swirls, so much need clamoring from the density of the *tsholnt. Yidish, zay zhe moykhl mayne grayzn.* Yiddish, forgive my blunders. *Mame-loshn, mayn grenetsland, ikh vel dir keyn mol nisht farlozn*/Yiddish, my borderland, I'll never abandon you. At home in the body. How did the poet come to land here, in this garret? How is meaning created within and beyond its sometimes narrow, sometimes expansive confines? Thus, the poet, single and indeed never married and now in late middle age, recalls and dissects foundational life events and moves through the world in conversation with those distant events, an urgent present, and imagined companionate figures.

As with most of my previous books, I find that I am most free—one of my primary goals when writing, and perhaps that of other poets and writers—when I am not focused solely on, tethered totally to, the autobiographical. "Free" ("Unanswered Questions Around the Endemic Bend")—like "peace" ("Milk and Honey Moon Harvest")—oft-bandied about, ever elusive. Still, I can breathe more easily, perhaps more fully even, when I am able to look within and outside the self during the creation of a given project. And moreover, the autobiographical is enriched by the fictional, and that each is mutually enhanced by the other. In some cases ("A Summons in Spring"), the past and the imagined intertwine in unexpected ways. Of course, the autobiographical itself is not always strictly autobiographical, but rather constructed and shaped to meet the dictates of the text at hand. Similarly, the fictional elements often spotlight, or otherwise illuminate, some the concerns and themes of the more identifiably autobiographical portions of the text. In reflecting upon this interplay, I'm reminded of how artists often create self-portraits, and how curators often include those in exhibitions devoted to their work. Seeing the artists' interpretation of self in juxtaposition with their interpretations of other souls and worlds allows for a deeper examination of each. One such example is the exhibition I saw in April 2024 at the Phillips Collection, Washington, D.C., devoted to Pierre Bonnard's work, which included several self-portraits. The sheer range of subjects throughout the exhibition—the bathers, the table below a window, the family enjoying an afternoon in the yard all so vividly rendered, so shimmering—and at the end, the images of the artist. The commitment to capturing the grand without, the courage to delve, dig within and bring forth whatever may be found there. Dazzling.

In contrast to some of my previous books, I have not divided the autobiographical and the imagined into two discrete parts. Instead, I intertwined these elements next to and through each other throughout the book as whole. I hope that this has created a valuable dissonance, perhaps an initially jagged but ultimately rewarding architecture that reflects the contents and the mood of the book itself.

In the book's first section, "Dawn's Dusk: Droplets Dotting Damask," some of the book's principal concerns are introduced. Here, family, identity, sexuality, and early/young-ish romance flicker. The mood is, not light exactly, but preliminary, exploratory. There is a sense of unfinishedness, of uncertainty. The poems don't exist in chronological order. In fact, the opposite is often the case. Poems about coming into adulthood ("What the Muzak Presaged … Provided" and "Siren Song Beyond the Physique Gardens") precede a poem on childhood ("The Babe's Legacy) and one that begins in childhood but ends elsewhere ("Crash Course in the Classics). The search for love and eros figures prominently in poems such as "City of Sweets," "Night of Seroconversion and Aftermath/Dialogue, in Eternal Embryo," and "Rendezvous Fantasia"). What hopefully lends this section some overall coherence is a sense of fluidity and becoming.

As its title suggests, "Black Blots Blast into Blue Baklava," the second section, brings a sense of greater forcefulness to the fore. Smooth damask is replaced by layers of dense baklava. In a culture literally predicated upon reproduction (peru u-revu/Be fruitful and multiply), the poet comes to terms with the fact that he will not be propagating and furthering the line ("Bebop Blues/Lullaby Ghost"). In two poems ("Milk and Honey Moon Harvest" and "Midrash on a Gravestone Acrostic Inscription"), the poet investigates the life of his mother and the words used to memorialize her. Questions of memorialization also haunt "What the Babushkas Saw" and self-memorialization in "At Last, A Celebration, Or, Improvisations on the Question of Inspiration." And too, the poet comes to explore the challenges ("Unanswered Questions Around the Endemic Bend" and "Water, Rising") and small victories ("Object Lessons/Treasure Retained") of late middle age.

Of course, as the book's subtitle states, not all of the pieces are poems, at least in how that designation is typically understood. Are they prose poems? Flash fiction? Hybrid pieces? Meditations? Arguably, the book includes all of these. When I write, I work to usher in that which is eager to emerge; I follow the muse. Rather than thinking about the precise format, I give voice to the concerns that I am investigating at that particular time. The muse guides the shape. But the muse allows dialogue, negotiation. Change, too. Heed the gentle muse!

And the garret. Not the attic. Not a place of hiding: Anne Frank and her family. Not a site of secrets: Gilbert and Gubar's madwoman in the attic. Rochester's first wife. But the garret. A place of independence, however fraught, however fragile, however off the "beaten" path. Windows onto sky and moon and dreams. Room for green, brown, and white. Prayer plants. Peace lilies. Possibility, too. A life lived on its own terms. A life of solitude, but not a life entirely alone. A life with tendrils and threads of connection. Still high, so many stairs, or sometimes even, a ladder. Could be precarious on the way up. Still hot, of course, close to the sun and so on. Only the roof as separation. Intervention ongoing against the elements. Still, a place of shelter and solitude and contemplation. Thank you for climbing the stairs. Mind the gap on your way down (and out).

—Yermiyahu Ahron Taub
Washington, D.C.

Acknowledgments

I am deeply grateful to the editors of the following publications in which these pieces, sometimes in different form and with different titles, first appeared:

Afn shvel (Spring-Summer 2024): "*Milkh-un-honikdike levone-harbstung*" (Yiddish version of "Milk and Honey Moon Harvest")

Amaranth Journal: A Journal of Food Writing, Art, & Design (Autumn 2024): "(Not Entirely) New World Rituals"

America's Future: An Anthology of Poetry and Prose (September 2025): "Activist's Retreat"

Amethyst Review: New Writing Engaged with the Sacred (August 19, 2024): "Three's a Minyan"

Asymptote Journal (July 2019): "Rendezvous Fantasia" and "Throne, With Cat" (English and Yiddish)

Beltway Poetry Quarterly (Fall 2019): "What the Babushkas Saw"

Capital Queer: A Pride Celebration from the Washington Writers' Publishing House (May 2025): "Permanent Resident, Without Green Card"

CCAR Journal: The Reform Jewish Quarterly (Winter 2025): "The Babe's Legacy"

Cigarette Fire Literary Magazine (Fall 2024): "Midrash on a Gravestone Acrostic Inscription" (English)

Cypress Review (September 30, 2024): "Entreaty" (English)

eMerge (Winter 2018): "Fellow Travelers" (English)

Exquisite Death (June 2024): "A Summons in Spring"

Hibiscus: The Poetry Vase (Issue 1): "City of Sweets," "Flaneur of the Fields," "Night of Seroconversion and Aftermath/Dialogue, in Eternal Embryo")

Magazine1 (Summer 2024): "Crash Course in the Classics"

The Mid-Atlantic Review (January 20, 2024): "Glass Dreams," "Mirage No. 2," and "Siesta's Sustenance"

The Mid-Atlantic Review (hard copy, 2024): "Siesta's Sustenance"

Sparks of Calliope: A Journal of Poetic Observations (November 24, 2024): "Ignorance, Bliss"

The Stygian Lepus Magazine (Issue Thirteen): "Ardor in and out of the Catacombs" and "Peace/Pieces of Mind"

This Is What America Looks Like: Washington Writers' Publishing House Anthology: Poetry & Fiction from DC, Maryland, Virginia (2021): "The Light at the Beginning of the Tunnel"

The Ulu Review (January 16, 2024): "Village Tableau, far from the Parade"

Yiddish Branzhe (January 2024): "Gebet" (Yiddish version of "Entreaty")

Yidishland: umophengike literarishe tsaytshrift (osyen 2020): "*Di likht baym onheyb funem tunel*" (Yiddish version of "The Light at the Beginning of the Tunnel")

Yidishland: umophengike literarishe tsaytshrift (osyen 2024): "*Midresh vegn a matseyve-akrostikh-aynshrift* (Yiddish verson of "Midrash on a Gravestone Acrostic Inscription")

I thank Miri Koral for editing of the Yiddish version of "Entreaty," "The Light at the Beginning of the Tunnel," "Rendezvous Fantasia," "Throne, With Cat," "Fellow Travelers," and "At Last, a Celebration, Or, Improvisations on the Question of Inspiration." Thank you to Gitl Schaechter-Viswanath for editing the Yiddish version of "Milk and Honey Moon Harvest" and to Velvl Chernin for editing the Yiddish version of "Midrash on a Gravestone Acrostic Inscription."

I thank Nancy Sack for so expertly proofreading the English portion of the manuscript.

I am grateful for a residency at the Rockvale Writers' Colony, College Grove, Tennessee (October 2023), where many of these poems were written. I offer thanks to Sandy Coomer, founder and director, and Heather Burch, assistant director, and to some of the writers in residence at the time: Karin Cox, Erika Dirk, Michele LaNoue, Ann Haley MacKenzie, Ann Rowson Love, Rebecca Marsh, Deborah Randolph, and Shannon Yarbrough, who offered fellowship and support.

Many thanks to Benjamin S. Grossberg, Barbara Krasner, Hiram Larew, Shara McCallum, and Elissa Ward for engaging so thoughtfully with my work and penning pre-publication words of support.

Thank you to Mimi David, Christen Kincaid, Leah Maines, and the entire team at Finishing Line Press for so gracefully shepherding this manuscript to publication.

Thank you to the friends and advocates whose love and encouragement courses through these pages: Andrew W.M. Beierle, Staffan Boos, Cindy Casey, Ellen Cassedy, Michael E. Gasper, Ken Giese, Pearl Gluck, Peter Goodman, James Hafner, Elizabeth Heaney, Miriam Isaacs, Howard Jaffe, Kate James and Scott Fontenot, Julia Spicher Kasdorf, Cecile Esther Kuznitz, Amos Lassen, Liz Lerner, Laura Levitt, Ashira Malka, Erin McGonigle, Ela Pelish, Nancy Sack, Yankl Salant, Paul Schaper, Faye-Ann Schott and Allen J. Frank, Jeffrey Shandler and Stuart Schear, Michael Swirsky, Phil Tavolacci, and Deidre Waxman.

Yermiyahu Ahron Taub is a poet and writer in English and Yiddish and a translator of Yiddish literature into English. He is the author of two books of fiction and six volumes of poetry, including *The Education of a Daffodil: Prose Poems/Di bildung fun a geln nartsis: prozelider* (2017). His translations from the Yiddish include *Dineh: An Autobiographical Novel* by Ida Maze (2022) and *Blessed Hands: Stories* by Frume Halpern (2023). Please visit his website at https://yataubdotnet.wordpress.com.

www.ingramcontent.com/pod-product-compliance
Lightning Source LLC
LaVergne TN
LVHW090613110826
845146LV00001B/370

* 9 7 9 8 8 9 9 9 0 4 1 7 2 *